begin with books

Columbia River

to the

Sacramento

By

CHARLES WILKES, U.S.N.

COMMANDER
UNITED STATES EXPLORING EXPEDITION
1839 TO 1842

1958
BIOBOOKS
OAKLAND 10, CALIFORNIA

California Relations #46

for

The International Geophysical Year

and

The Centennial of the State of Oregon

FOREWORD

All things considered, this may be the most interesting document ever produced relating to the exploration and acquisition of Western America, for the reader it reveals the territory covered and the people interviewed better than any other report known to this writer. For our copy we use the edition printed at Philadelphia in 1845 by Lea and Blanchard.

From what we can find, this was the first published account of what is now Highway 99, the North-South road of the Southern Pacific Railroad and the line of the airplanes, it was in use by the Hudson Bay fur hunters and heavily used by the Oregon Gold Rushers (both ways) and the Concord stages, it still is the most fascinating, picturesque and scenic highroad in the world, the Gateway to Western Canada and Alaska, to Mt. Rainier and the Grand Coulee, Olympic Peninsula, Astoria and the Columbia basin, Mt. Hood, the 3 Sisters and Crater Lake, Mt. Shasta and Lassen Park, The Cascades and Sierra, Lake Tahoe, The Yosemite, Big Trees and Parks, Death Valley and Mt. Whitney, La Brea Deposits and the Salton Sea.

Our author, Charles Wilkes, born in New York, navy midshipman in 1818, first to use astronomical instruments for observation, 1838, he sailed from Norfolk in command of a squadron to explore the South Seas, 1839, he was the earliest to name and chart the Antarctic Continent, in 1841 he visited, by direction, the Northwestern Coast of America, returning by the Cape of Good Hope to New York in 1842.

He was in command of the steamer "San Jacinto" in 1861. Intercepted at sea the English mail-steamer "Trent," brought off the Confederate commissioners, John Slidell and James Mason, taking them to Boston harbor. The Navy Department gave him an emphatic commendation, Congress a resolution of thanks. His act caused great rejoicing throughout the north, where he was the hero of the hour. For his services to science as an explorer he received a gold medal from the Geographical Society of London.

Here we like to emphasize Wilkes as an agent of his government, other nations were represented in the territory, under today's standard he might be writing *Inside Western America*, rivals were present and reporting to English, French and Russian capitals, he, you will note, covered much ground, was well received from Vancouver Fort to Santa Clara. He at the same time interviewed almost every worthwhile and important person he met in his travels, all of this was in due time delivered along the Potomac.

Wilkes' party was the first to raise the American Flag west of the Rockies, in what is now the State of Washington, celebrating the Fourth of July with a barbecue no less, a symbol, a gesture that they were at home, we, however direct your attention to the report as a whole, and what followed its reception by the Congress shortly after the expedition reached the East Coast, its printing was limited to one hundred copies and studied carefully by the leaders of government, Benton, Polk, as well as by other expansionists, timely, because of the Texas accession, it may have started the Fremont exploration, it surely influenced and strengthened the western men, this report was the catalyst that, with the next Presidential election in a period of four years from its receipt, increased the territory of the United States by fifty per cent or more, for it added to the Union all west of the mountains, Oregon, Washington, Idaho, Utah, Nevada, California, Arizona, New Mexico. It resulted in the purchase of Alaska and the adding of Hawaii. The third and final thrust, The Revolution, the Louisiana Purchase, and the West, all incidentally heavily influenced by Jefferson and his ardent disciples. All in all a significant and remarkable contribution to the history of the Great West.

One authority states "the greatest exploring trip in the history of this Country," Hobbs points out, that Wilkes was the first to explore a stretch of Antarctic Coast long enough to prove its Continental character. On orders signed by J. K. Paulding, Secretary of the Navy, ". . . Thence you will direct your course to the Northwest Coast of America, making such surveys and examinations, first of the Territory of the United States on the seaboard, and of the Columbia river, and afterwards along the coast of California, with special reference to the Bay of San Francisco." On the way the squadron visited Fiji and spent six months in the Hawaiian Islands, proceeding they reached the Strait of Juan de Fuca in May 1841, on land they were extended hospitality at Fort Vancouver by Dr. McLaughlin and Mr. Douglass, a reception if possible even more hearty was given the party on its arrival at New Helvetia, Captain Sutter offering everything at his command, after a two-day visit Sutter added "a wish that the day was not far distant when the stars and stripes would wave over this Country."

Here reproduced are very early plates of Shasta and the Marysville Buttes, the latter put us on search, which resulted in the folding map herewith. We found the map of Hyacinth Farm in the Public Library at Willows, a gift to the library by Mr. Heil, vice-president and manager of the Kern County Title Co., it may be the only known copy. The original Ide Map has not been uncovered, however, the approval of the farm grant in the original is privately held in Willows, signed by Buchanan, the Lyman Map attest is quite old, the then owner of the property, Dr. McKee, was a property owner in Colusa County and married Josefa De Soto, owner of Capoy Rancho and likely Jacinto, (it is presently in the Jacinto School District). McKee, Latin scholar?, named it Hyacinth?. From the Farm (rancho) is visible the Buttes and ₁close by the campsite of the party responsible for the picture included within. In the County Recorder's office at Willows there is a later, larger wall map of Glenn County showing the Hyacinth (Jacinto) to be owned by Dr. Glenn. The whole appearance bears more than name only a remarkable resemblance to the battlefield near Houston, flat country, Sacramento, Buffalo Bayou, it is presently in active use by dairymen. This whole region is well used in season by pheasant hunters. Our Survey Map is by permission of the librarian, Miss Elizabeth Eubanks, a very keen and fine active student of Glenn County history. A Mexican vara is equivalent to 33 inches.

Dr. Hugh J. Glenn, Viriginian, Veteran of the Mexican War, under General Price with the First Missouri Regiment, a 49er and successful miner on the American River, acquiring the Jacinto Grant and adjacent property to Sixty-Five thousand acres. He was termed the "Largest farmer in the World." Forty-five thousand acres were used in the cultivation of wheat, in one year the harvest ran to fifty million pounds of grain, on the property and the river he built an elaborate home, also the town of Jacinto with hotel, ferry and numerous dwellings for his help, maintained a public school, and over two thousand head of horses and mules.

Jos A. Sullivan
November 23, 1958

515 Weldon Avenue
Oakland 10, California

In this we continue our dedication to great Seamen and Explorers and find ourselves delighted to honor

JUAN RODRIGUES CABRILLO

who, on September 28, 1542, landed on the Coast of California at San Diego, just within fifty years from Columbus' landfall on the Atlantic side of the continent.

Probably of Portuguese birth, he served under Narvaez, in the conquest of Mexico "a very capable man," later Captain in Guatemala under Governor Alvarado, always in the service of Spain. Mendoza, Viceroy of New Spain, having sent Coronado overland, directed Cabrillo along the West Coast, this he gave diligent attention and during several months sailed as far north as to sight Mt. St. Helena, snow-covered in Winter, a very great effort on an unknown coast, in small ships, under very trying conditions of wind and water. Returning South he, in landing on one of the islands of the Coast, broke a bone and in a few days was dead and buried in California. A great Captain, he accomplished his instructions and made the Great Sacrifice; no explorer on the Pacific could do more.

CHAPTER I.

CONTENTS

1

COLUMBIA RIVER.

1841.

he Vincennes having sailed, I at once set about preparing for the survey of the river. I found that, agreeably to my first instructions, Captain Hudson had lost no time in despatching the parties for the interior, but the orders I had sent by Mr. Waldron, arrested their progress. I issued these orders because I anticipated that it would be necessary to make some change in the route they were to pursue; and in the mean time they would have more opportunity to prepare them selves for the journey.

Finding that Mr. Dana had not set out for the interior, I now saw and regretted the necessity of countermanding the orders for the party that was destined for the Rocky Mountains.

The boats of the Peacock were ordered to be fully manned and fitted out with all the requisites for surveying duties, and officers attached to each.

On the morning of the 9th, we began the survey. Some time had been before spent in taking a few angles and soundings, but with so little success, that I rejected the whole. The weather proved unfavourable for any of our operations, except that of putting up signals. We encamped at night on the small sandy island in the centre of the bay, where we were very uncomfortable, for the sand flew about and covered every thing. In the morning we had a thick fog, when I determined to go to Baker's Bay, where we could obtain water; for that of the Columbia is not fresh as low down as this point.

We found the tide exceedingly strong, and having some apprehensions that the boats might lose their way, I thought it better for us to make for the Chinook shore, and follow it until we reached the cape. It may seem strange that this precaution should be taken, but it is necessary at all times, even in clear weather; for the tide is frequently so strong, that it cannot be stemmed by oars; and too much caution cannot be observed in passing across the bay. As little frequented as it is, many accidents have occurred to boats and canoes, by their being swept by the tide into the breakers on the bar, where all hands have perished. The Indians are very cautious, and it is only at certain times of the tide that they will attempt to make the passage.

We reached Baker's Bay in two hours, and formed our encampment; and here we determined to remain until the weather should become clear, and allow us to proceed with our duties.

As no news had been received from Passed Midshipman Eld's party, whom it will be recollected, I had despatched from Nisqually to Gray's Harbour, by the Chickeeles, and as the time for which he had provisions had expired, I became apprehensive lest some accident might have detained him. I therefore despatched Lieutenant De Haven and Acting-Master Baldwin, with a few Indians, along the coast to Gray's Harbour, which is about forty miles distant, to convey a supply of provisions for that party, and to bring intelligence of them. This duty was executed by these gentlemen with promptness, and they reported that the party was struggling with difficulties of no ordinary character, of which I shall have occasion to speak hereafter.

RAMSEY.   GEORGE.

The weather continued rainy and cold; but this did not seem to trouble our native pilots, Ramsey and his brother George. While we were preparing our huts, these men were seen upon the bank, deliberately stripping off their clothes, which they carefully folded up, and placed upon the ground for pillows; they then lay down, and covering themselves with a blanket, slept as sound as if on beds of down. I happened to see them arising in the morning, and they appeared refreshed and perfectly content, although it had rained hard all night.

These men were exceedingly fond of rum, the hope of obtaining which, when the daily ration was served out, was the great inducement that led them to accompany our parties.

These two were good specimens of the Flathead Indians, and I was therefore pleased at having an opportunity of sketching them with the camera lucida, of which sketches the cuts on the opposite page are copies.

Before I reached Astoria, Captain Varney, of the brig Thomas H. Perkins, had proposed to sell his vessel to the government, provided he could arrange his affairs with Dr. M'Laughlin. I now learned that Dr. M'Laughlin had arrived at Astoria, for which place I set out in the afternoon, in company with Captain Hudson. We embarked in the tender, but after proceeding some distance, we found it impossible to reach Astoria. We therefore returned to Baker's Bay, which we had some difficulty in reaching.

The next day we succeeded in reaching Astoria, and found that the arrangements for the purchase of the brig could be effected, and I therefore bought her for the United States for nine thousand dollars, after having her thoroughly examined by the carpenters of the squadron. On taking possession of this brig, I changed her name to that of "the Oregon."

This acquisition released me from much anxiety, by providing accommodations for the crew of the Peacock, and at the same time affording a suitable vessel to continue the operations of the squadron. Captain Hudson took charge of the Oregon, and the alterations necessary to adapt her for this service were at once commenced. After making these arrangements, Dr. M'Laughlin departed for Vancouver. He gave a passage to Messrs. Hale and Dana, Messrs. Peale and Rich having previously gone up the river. These gentlemen had already visited the country around the mouth of the Columbia, every opportunity having been afforded them by Captain Hudson. Several of the officers visited the mountain ranges, but did not succeed in ascending the highest peaks.

During the occupation of Astoria by the Expedition, the place became quite civilized-looking, in comparison to what it was on my first arrival, and a mart for all the commodities of the country. Besides our own men, there were many Indians to be seen lounging and moving about, seeking employment, or with some small articles to sell.

Short excursions were made by many of us in the vicinity, and one of these was to visit the primeval forest of pines in the rear of Astoria, a sight well worth seeing. Mr. Drayton took a camera lucida drawing of one of the largest trees, which the opposite plate is engraved from. It conveys a good idea of the thick growth of the trees, and is quite characteristic of this forest. The soil on which this timber grows is rich and fertile, but the obstacles to the agriculturist are almost insuperable. The largest tree of the sketch was thirty-nine feet six inches in circumference, eight feet above the ground, and had a bark eleven inches thick. The height could not be ascertained, but it was thought to be upwards of two hundred and fifty feet, and the tree was perfectly straight.

It was the season of the fishery when the Peacock was wrecked, and the Kilamukes, Clatsops, and Chinooks, were collected in the neighbourhood. Many of these came with their families, and took up their abode near Astoria; for it costs them little trouble to move all their worldly goods. They generally had for sale salmon, venison, sturgeon, moccasins, and mats.

When the crew first landed, eight or ten salmon might be bought for a cotton shirt, or its value in red or green baize; but the Indians soon found that higher prices might be obtained for the asking, and before our departure from the Columbia river, the price was enhanced one-half.

The vicious propensities of the Indians were seen here, as they appear around all the posts of the Hudson Bay Company, or where strangers are encamped: gambling is the vice to which they are most prone. Both sexes are equally filthy, and I am inclined to believe will continue so; for their habits are inveterate, and from all the accounts I could gather from different sources, there is reason to believe that they have not improved or been benefited by their constant intercourse with the whites, except in a very few cases. It is indeed probable that the whole race will be extinguished ere long, from the natural effects of their mode of life, even if no pestilential disease should come among them to sweep them off in a single season.

I saw more of their gambling here, and the lengths to which they carry it, than in any other place, in consequence of having occasion to come oftener in contact with them. The game most practised was played by one of them concealing two small sticks in the hand so adroitly as to elude scrutiny, while the others guessed which hand contained them. Two parties play at this, sitting upon different sides of a large board; and whilst the concealment of the stick is going on, they keep up a kind of chaunt and beating with the sticks, to produce confusion and noise, in order to distract the attention of the players. The air they sing is—

Drawn by A. T. Agate.

ASTORIA, COLUMBIA RIVER.

Engraved by Rawdon, Wright & Hatch.

Wa - - - - - ich   e - e   Wa - - - -

ich   e - e   Wa - ich   Wa - ich.

This game seems to amuse them, not only for hours but for whole nights, and the great cause of excitement lies in the stakes. Ten is game, and the party lose or win two at each guess.

They have another sport, which seemed to be the favourite with the Indians around Vancouver: this is played with a number of disks of bone or ivory, of the size of a quarter of a dollar, one of which differs from the rest. These are concealed in tow or fibrous hemp, and the guessing takes place in the same way. With these disks the players make a great noise by shaking them in their hands. There is great attention required in those who venture to play the game; and such appears to be its fascination, that I have seen them deprive themselves of one garment or article after another, until they were entirely destitute; and it is even said they often stake the freedom, not only of themselves, but of their children.

At Astoria we saw one day, when there was quite a crowd of Indians at the encampment, several squaws, all dressed in their best attire. These were all more than usually attentive to their personal appearance. The principal among them was a widow, whose time of mourning for the death of her husband had just expired. Her object was to notify her friends that she was ready to receive the addresses of any one who was in want of a wife. To give such notification was, as I found on inquiry, a common custom among the Chinooks.

The widow was of masculine make, and what we would call a buxom dame. She was attended by seven others, of small stature in comparison, who were her maids, and all evidently accompanied her to do honour to the occasion. Every half hour they would arrange themselves in a row, and the widow at their head, affecting a modest downcast look, would commence a chaunt, informing the bystanders that her period of mourning was out, that she had forgotten her deceased husband, given her grief to the winds, and was now ready to espouse another. This chaunt was accompanied by a small movement of the feet and body, which, with the gutteral song and consequent excitement of such an exhibition, caused the fair ones to wax so warm that the perspiration rolled down their painted cheeks; this, with the crimson flush, all tended to add brilliancy to their dark eyes, as they were now and then cast around upon the multitude of Indians, who seemed all admiration. I did not ascertain whether the fair one succeeded in winning a second husband, but I am satisfied that her exertions were such as ought to have obtained her one.

The Chinook and Kilamuke tribes entertain, as I was informed, the idea of a future state, in their hunting-grounds, which, in their language, they call Tamath. The road to them is supposed to be difficult, and none but those who are of good character can go there, by the road which is called O-tu-i-huti, a term by which they designate the Via Lactea. They have a strong belief that all their departed relatives and friends have a guard over them, and prevent evil from approaching them. Each Indian has his tamanuus, or spirit, which is selected by him at a very early age, and is generally the first object they see in going out to the woods, that has animal life. Others create from their imagination one that has never met mortal eyes. The choice of a spirit, however, insignificant it may appear, has a great influence on their after-life; for, by its supposed commands, they are directed to good or evil, as they conceive that a nonconformity to its wishes would involve them in a multitude of evils, for they suppose it is able to destroy health, or preserve it, or inflict miseries without end.

They at times, and particularly when in the water, pretend to hold converse with it, and talk to themselves in a low, monotonous tone of voice.

Ikaui is the name of their most powerful god: to him they ascribe the creation of all things. A mountain is called after him, from its being supposed that he was there turned into stone, and they point out the principal rock, which rises in a pyramidal shape, as his statue.

They believe that their departed friends and relatives have a knowledge of what is going on among the living; and they, in consequence, will not eat in sight of the dead, nor laugh, for fear their mouths will be turned askew. With the dead, they bury, as in other parts of Oregon, their guns, knives, pots, and kettles; and I was informed that these articles would not be stolen when thus deposited. I presume, however, that such is not the fact, for I observed that these things had always been previously rendered useless, by either being burnt, or having holes punched through them, in order to take away the temptation of theft. Formerly, slaves were not unfrequently killed at a chief's funeral, in order to bury them with their masters. They speak of the dead walking at night, when they are supposed to awake, and get up to search for food. They have many superstitions, that have been already noticed, of which that relating to the salmon is the most singular, and the most strictly adhered to.

The god who made the Columbia river, and all the fish in it, they call Italupus. He taught their ancestors how to procure fire, make nets, and catch fish. The first salmon caught are all tabooed, and they dare not sell them; they must all be cut up and cooked the day they are caught. A dog must never be permitted to eat the heart of a salmon; and in order to prevent this, they cut the heart of the fish out before they sell it.

Italupus is supposed to nourish the salmon, and cause them to be abundant during the whole summer, that they may lay up their store of it for the winter.

Having completed all the arrangements, and the weather becoming fine, on the 16th we resumed our duties in the survey, which was now carried on with spirit. The stations being established, and the triangulation completed, the tender, with two boats, was left to sound out the bay, while the remaining part of the force was moved up the river, to continue the surveys, in company with the Porpoise and Oregon; for I now found it necessary that both vessels should proceed up to Vancouver. This was not only to insure a more thorough outfit for the Oregon, but it also served to forward the surveying duties, and to afford the officers and men such quarters at night as would protect them from the sickly season, that was approaching, and of which we had received such unfavourable accounts. The plan adopted for the survey of this river will be given in the Hydrographical Memoir.

On the 18th of August, I left Astoria, with the Porpoise and Oregon, to continue the survey. We reached Tongue Point, where we anchored, previously to crossing thence to the opposite side of the river, through the crooked channel which was then believed to be the only passage by which a vessel of any class could ascend the stream.*

On the 19th, the vessels attempted to pass through this channel, but on entering it they both took the ground. The tide was at its full height and soon began to fall, when the Porpoise began to keel over, until she fell on her beam-ends. We were in hopes that the night tide would be sufficient to float her off, but we found its rise less by nearly a foot than that of the day; it therefore became necessary to make extraordinary exertions to prepare for the next day's tide by buoying

---

* A channel which we afterwards discovered leads directly upwards from Tongue Point, and affords every desirable facility for the navigation of the Columbia river.

her up with casks, which, fortunately, we had at hand, on board the Oregon. It now became necessary to float her off, in order to avoid a second failure. We therefore had recourse to passing her chain cable under her bottom, to which a line of casks was lashed on the weather side, at the same time the launch was suspended as a weight from her masthead to preserve her in the same position. The hawsers that had been landed at Astoria by our store-vessels were sent for and attached to the brig's anchors, and so placed as to haul her at once into the deepest water and through the narrow pass. When all was prepared, a strong wind arose from the seaward, and caused a swell which broke adrift some of the casks, leaving sufficient, however, to float her before high water.

I was much relieved when I saw her again afloat, for I had felt not a little anxious lest in the drifting sands of the river she might have formed a bed, which would have placed it out of our power to get her off before the next spring tides, and would have compelled us to discharge all her guns, &c. Although this would have been attended with a great deal of trouble, it would have been of little consequence compared with the loss of time, which we could ill afford to spare.

After getting her off, we ran up the river a few miles, and anchored just below the Pillar Rock, and opposite to Waikaikum. Waikaikum belongs to a chief named Skamakewea, and is a large lodge, picketed around with planks.

Mr. Hale passed two days there, and obtained much interesting information from him relative to his tribe. This chief formerly had a large tribe under him, but since the year 1830 the fever has destroyed them nearly all. The portion of this country more immediately affected by this scourge, extends along the banks of the river from the ocean to the Cascades; but that part of it which is within the influence of the ocean tides, is the least subject to its ravages. When an Indian contracts this disease, he seldom recovers, for the treatment he goes through is sufficient to kill a person in good health.

Pillar Rock is called by the Indians Taluaptea, after the name of a chief, who in bygone days lived at the falls of the Columbia, and who, having incurred the displeasure of their spirit, called Talapos, was turned into a rock, and placed where he would be washed by the waters of the great river. The rock is twenty-five feet high, and only ten feet square at its top: it is composed of conglomerate or pudding-stone, and is fast crumbling to pieces. I found great difficulty in ascending it.

The next morning, in proceeding up the river to carry on the survey, one of the small boats of the Porpoise, that we had in tow, was, through the negligence of her crew, capsized. Every thing in her except her oars was lost, and in addition to this the accident caused us much detention.

In the afternoon we reached Katalamet Point, and anchored at the lower end of Puget Island, where we passed the next day (Sunday). On Monday we again resumed our surveying duties, and reached Oak Point, where the river takes a turn to the southward and eastward. On the 24th, Lieutenant Emmons joined me, and received his instructions to pass through the country to the south, and join the ship at San Francisco. His instructions will be found in Appendix IV. Just before reaching Walker's Island we ran aground, by the pilot mistaking his marks, but were soon relieved. In the evening of the next day, we reached Mount Coffin, at the mouth of the Cowlitz. This mount afforded a favourable point for astronomical observations, being seven hundred and ten feet high, and quite isolated. The canoes used by the Indians as coffins are seen upon it in every direction, in all stages of decay. They are supported between trees, at the height of four or five feet above the ground, and about them are hung the utensils that had belonged to the deceased, or that had been offered as tokens of respect.

I remained the whole day on the top of this mount, and obtained a full set of observations; the weather being remarkably clear and beautiful. Here my boat's crew carelessly omitted to extinguish the fire they had used for cooking our dinner, and as we were pulling off to the brig, I regretted to see that the fire had spread, and was enveloping the whole area of the mount; but there was no help for it. The fire continued to rage throughout the night, until all was burnt. I took the earliest opportunity of explaining to the Indians who were in the neighbourhood, that the fire was accidental; and, after receiving a few small presents, they appeared satisfied that it was so. But a few years earlier, the consequence of such carelessness would have been a hostile attack, that might have involved us in difficulty of no ordinary kind. We had a minor punishment to undergo, for the smoke was so great that it enveloped all the signals towards the mouth of the river, and made it necessary for me to anchor within sight of Mount Coffin till the next morning.

Before reaching the mouth of the Willamette, better known here as the Wapautoo Branch, a long flat extends across the river, where we were again unfortunately detained a few hours, by getting aground. Warrior's Point, the locality where Mr. Wyeth proposed to erect his great city of the west, was passed; and on the 28th, at sunset, we anchored off Vancouver. Here we found that Sir George Simpson had arrived over-land from Canada, on a tour of inspection, and on his way to visit the Russian settlement at Sitka. The next morning we had a visit from him, accompanied by Dr. M'Laughlin, Mr. Douglass, Mr. Rowan, and Mr. Von Freeman, of the Russian Company.

Sir George Simpson left England the preceding month of March, and was to return thither by way of Kamtschatka: a journey which he hoped to perform in less than two years. He had seen much service while acting as an officer of the Hudson Bay Company, from which he has retired, and in which he now holds no share. Since his retirement, he is employed by the stockholders of the Company, as the inspector of all the departments, and to report upon the state of the trading posts; this leaves him free to act without prejudice.

The mode of apportioning the profits of the Company is as follows: after a certain per centage is paid to the stockholders who own the capital, the surplus is divided among the active partners, including the chief factor, traders, &c.: who are thus all interested in the profits arising from their own exertions. In order that Sir George Simpson may be impartial in adjusting and reporting on the affairs, he receives a salary of two thousand pounds a year. Sir George has been lately knighted, for projecting and superintending the outfits of the voyage of his nephew, who completed the discoveries in the north, and the history of whose melancholy end has become so well known to all interested in Arctic discoveries.

Captain Hudson, the officers, and myself, were invited to partake of a formal dinner at Vancouver: on this occasion, all the functionaries of the Company were present, and each individual seemed to have his place assigned him. It reminded me of the description of a feast of feudal times, for there were many "below the salt."

Like all great dinners, it was stiff and formal. Sir George Simpson occupied the head of the table, and there were none but men present. Their wives seem to be little thought of, but for what reason I could not imagine, as many of them were highly worthy of notice. Their frequent exertions in protecting the settlements and their husbands, show a devotion to them and their interests, that is highly commendable; and why they should not be treated as their equals, I am at a loss to conceive. They will bear an advantageous comparison with any others who have had so few opportunities. Those whom I saw exhibited both propriety of behaviour and modesty of deportment. It may perhaps be that their seclusion from mixed society is their own choice; but such a regulation cannot but tend to prevent improvement, and retard advancement in civilization.

The Columbia river was now very different in appearance from what it had been in the month of June. The stream was confined within it narrowest limits, and was nineteen feet below high-water mark.

The Indians were now encamped on the strands, over which the volume of water had rushed, in its swollen state, with irresistible force. Vancouver exhibited the aspects of an extensive farming establishment, with its well-stored granaries, stacks of grain, &c. All showed that the crops had been plentiful, and gave ample proof of the industry and success of agriculture.

Soon after the wreck of the Peacock, Captain Hudson, hearing that Dr. M'Laughlin was in want of hands to aid him in the harvest, despatched the Kanakas belonging to the Peacock up to Vancouver, to assist in gathering it. It afforded some little pleasure to contribute this aid, and thus in some small degree to repay the attentions and kindness of the Company's officers.

While at Vancouver, my time was taken up by the astronomic and magnetic observations. The former gave its position in longitude 122° 39′ 34·6″ W., and latitude 45° 36′ 53″ N.

Having understood, from the gentlemen at Vancouver, that both Mr. David Douglas and Captain Belcher had found some discrepancies in their magnetic observations, which were quite unaccountable; and as they had experimented within the fort, I determined to make mine in my tent, on the banks of the river, where no apparent local attraction existed. There were, notwithstanding, some irregularities which I could not account for.

While I was thus engaged, Captain Hudson carried on the repairs of the Oregon with great rapidity. The articles necessary for this purpose which we ourselves were not able to supply, were cheerfully furnished us, at reasonable prices, from the stores and workshops of the Company. Indeed, nothing could exceed the kind attentions that were lavished upon us; and the moment we expressed a desire, it was immediately complied with.

On the 1st of September, Passed Midshipmen Eld and Colvocoressis, with Mr. Brackenridge and party, arrived. Orders were immediately given for them to join Lieutenant Emmons's party, on the Willamette; and they were finally despatched on the tour through to California.

It will be remembered that Passed Midshipmen Eld and Colvocoressis were ordered to make a journey through the Chickeeles country, to Gray's Harbour, just as the ship was getting under way from Nisqually, and that circumstances rendered their departure more hurried than it was desirable it should be. But through the kindness of Mr. Anderson and Captains M'Niel and Scarborough, the party was not left in want of any thing very material.

The party under command of Mr. Eld, consisted of Passed Midshipman Colvocoressis, Mr. Brackenridge, Sergeant Stearns, privates Rodgers and Dinsman, John Brooks (seaman), Thomas Ford and Henry Waltham (ordinary seamen), with a half-breed boy, named Joe, who was to act as their interpreter.

They left Nisqually on the 19th of July, and proceeded towards one of the southwest arms of Puget Sound (of which we had but a few days before finished the survey) in two canoes, that had been purchased. They were sorry craft, but better could not be procured, and Mr. Eld was not disposed to delay on account of imaginary difficulties. His instructions will be found in Appendix XIV., Vol. IV.

I had told him he might be absent for forty days on his own resources, as I calculated he would, by the assistance of the Indians, be able to obtain both fish and game. I also enjoined upon him great attention to economy in the use of his provisions.

On the same evening, he arrived within a short distance of the portage; and the next morning Mr. Colvocoressis went, with the sergeant and boy, to an old squaw chief, who had promised, at Nisqually, to be their guide to the Sachal river, and to furnish horses and men to cross the portage. They returned at an early hour, without either horses or Indians, but with a promise that they were to be furnished the next day. The next morning they found that the chief had arrived, with five horses and a number of Indians, and was ready to transport the baggage. Some time, however, elapsed before an arrangement could be made for the large canoe, which was thought to be too heavy to transport; but this was finally settled by the same personage offering another in lieu of it, which, though of smaller dimensions, was accepted. Ten Indians were furnished to transport it and the rest of the articles, and they were soon in a condition to move. This despatch was principally owing to the directions and management of the squaw chief, who seemed to exercise more authority than any that had been met with; indeed, her whole character and conduct placed her much above those around her. Her horses were remarkably fine animals; her dress was neat, and her whole establishment bore the indications of Indian opulence. Although her husband was present, he seemed under such good discipline, as to warrant the belief that the wife was the ruling power, or, to express it in more homely language, "wore the breeches."

The portage was easily accomplished: it passes through a forest of lofty spruce and maple trees, with an undergrowth of common hazel and spiræa; its length was four miles. The soil was composed of a shallow, black, sandy, vegetable earth.

On their route they passed three small prairies, one of which was about ten acres in extent, and lay on the northwest side of a lake: the lake, called Sachal by the Indians, was examined, and found to be one and a half miles in length, and three-fourths of a mile in breadth. It is surrounded on all sides by willow and alders; the soil about it was a light brown sandy loam; the forest extends down to the water, which is of a dark brown colour, as if tinged with vegetable matter; this, however, was not the case, for in taking the water up in a glass, it was found pure and crystal-like.

A line of soundings was taken across the lake, by which five and a quarter fathoms was found to be the greatest depth. It was said to abound in fish, but they did not succeed in taking any. In the lake were quantities of yellow lilies (Nuphar lutea), pond-weed (Potamogeton) of two species, and a water-lily (Nymphæa).

Mr. Eld was told that there was another lake to the northeast, and set out with Mr. Colvocoressis, to visit it. The supposed lake was reached after a walk of five miles over the same kind of country, and proved to be only a pond, about two hundred yards in diameter, quite shallow, and covered, like the former, with water-lilies.

After their return they broke up the encampment, and embarking in their canoes on Lake Sachal, passed to its southern end, where they entered the river of the same name. This appeared at first almost impassable, for it was for four miles almost choked up with Sparganiums, Nuphars, &c., so that it was difficult to pass even with the small canoe. Its breadth was from twenty to sixty feet, and it was from three to twelve feet deep. The turns were sometimes so short, that the large canoe would be in contact with the thickets on the banks at both ends, and it required much force to drag her along, by pulling by the branches, and caused great labour in cutting their way. They also unfortunately lost their hatchet, which afterwards proved a serious mishap.

They were obliged to continue their course down the river until nine o'clock at night, before they could find any place to encamp, on account of the bog and jungle. At that hour they came to a small green spot, occupied by a party of Indians. Here Mr. Eld obtained some altitudes of the north star for latitude; and the next day, being compelled to make a portage of two miles to avoid an impassable part of the river, he employed himself, during the time it was making, in getting a full set of equal altitudes. By 6 P. M. they had carried every thing across and embarked; but the river was full of sand-bars, shallow rapids, and sunken snags, which often compelled them to drag the canoe over by main force. The land on both sides of the river is flat, marshy, and well wooded. Among the trees were many ash. They stopped for the night at an Indian camp. Mr. Eld endeavoured to induce the old chief to accompany him down the river; but he declined, assigning as a reason that he was afraid of the Chinooks. He boasted that he was the chief of the Sachal tribe; but as the party had met with but two or three other Indians during the route, they were at a loss to know where the tribe resided.

On the 24th, they again embarked on the river, and had another fatiguing day; but being now provided with poles, they succeeded better in navigating the canoe. When they had proceeded some distance, they were overtaken by the squaw chief and her husband, who passed them quickly in a light canoe. During the day they saw several deserted native huts, situated on small prairies, extending back some distance from the river, and in the rear, on either side, were seen hills rising to the height of about fifteen hundred feet. No kind of rock had been observed on their route, except a single block of granite, which was passed on one of the prairies near Lake Sachal. The weather, for the few last days, had been fine and clear.

On the 25th, they set out at an early hour, and in passing one of the rapids in the large canoe, it came in contact with a snag, which tore off part of the gunwale, and half filled the canoe with water. At ten o'clock they reached the place where the Sachal enters the Chickeeles, which is there one hundred and fifty feet wide, and runs with a rapid current. The bottom was gravelly, and the surface smooth, except where a sand and gravel bar stretched across the river, in a direction about east-northeast. One lonely Indian was met at the junction, from whom they bought some pieces of dried elk.

The soil on both sides of the river, for about one-third of a mile back, was a deep, rich, alluvial loam, overgrown with poplar, willow, dogwood, and alder, with an undergrowth of raspberry. On the 26th, the old chief joined the party, and they all proceeded down the river together, to the point where the Kluckullum enters the Chickeeles, where they halted. No inducement could prevail upon the chief to serve as a guide up the Sachap, another branch of the Chickeeles.

In the afternoon they encamped at the mouth of the Sachap, and Mr. Eld made preparations to set out early the next morning, to explore it, having obtained a guide from among the Indians they met with at a fishing station in the vicinity. No fish, however, were to be procured, but on their descent they came upon several large flocks of teal, out of which Mr. Brackenridge killed four.

At an early hour on the 27th, Mr. Eld, Sergeant Stearns, and two men, set out on their jaunt up the Sachap, in a small canoe. About eight miles from the camp they came to the place where the river forks, forming the Sachap and Tarqucorau; here they took horses, and proceeded eight miles farther, in a northeasterly direction, and encamped in a small prairie. Neither of the two rivers is penetrable by a canoe, so overgrown and choked up are they with bushes and bogs. Just at sunset they passed a party of Suquamish Indians, who were very anxious that Mr. Eld should encamp with them; but this he declined doing, and preferred passing some distance beyond.

On the morning of the 28th, they again started at an early hour, and passed through a very rough and apparently little frequented country. The guide had much difficulty in finding his way through a forest which the fire had partly consumed. At 9^h 30^m they recrossed the Sachap, which was there a small brook, about twenty feet wide, coming from a northwest direction. It was but knee-deep, and clogged with large logs and trees. Shortly after passing this stream, the country grew so rough that it was impossible to proceed farther with the horses, and the guide told Mr. Eld that he would be obliged to leave them. As no notice of this difficulty in the route had been previously given, it was natural for Mr. Eld to suspect that his guide was forming some scheme to deceive him, and go off with his property. Deeming it proper to come to a right understanding, and to make the guide aware that he was on the look-out to punish any attempt at fraud, he led the chief aside, and told him that he intended to hold him responsible in case of the loss of any of his things, or of his being deceived. He then ordered him to leave one of his slaves in charge of the horses and effects until their return. This was accordingly done, and they proceeded on foot for Lake Nanvitz, which they reached by one o'clock. This proved to be a fine sheet of water, a mile and a half long, by three-fourths of a mile wide, surrounded by a thick forest of pines. Here they found an Indian family hunting, who had just killed an elk, of which Mr. Eld procured the greater part, for a small quantity of powder and shot. These were also of the Suquamish tribe. The old man of this party spoke of another lake, not far distant, to which he took Mr. Eld. This was no more than about half the size of the former, and the name the Indians gave it was Kamalatiz: it had much the same character as the larger one. There was no opportunity of getting the depth of these two lakes, for want of a canoe. Neither of them has an outlet. From the Indians' account, the Sachap takes its rise in a small pond to the northwest of these lakes.

Having accomplished the object he had in view, Mr. Eld turned back, and soon reached the place where they had left the horses and articles, which they found all safe, under the charge of the slave, who, from appearances, had not moved from his position during the time of their absence, and was much relieved at their return.

The next day they returned to their party on the Chickeeles, passing on their route some of the gigantic pine trees, so often to be met with in this territory. Some of these had been burnt, and had in consequence fallen; Mr. Eld thus had an opportunity of measuring them. One, that was not selected as the largest, for there were many of equal if not greater length and diameter, was measured, and the part that lay in one piece was found to be two hundred feet long; another piece of the same tree was twenty-five feet long, and at the small end of the latter, it was still ten inches in diameter. Allowing twelve feet for the portion destroyed by fire, Mr. Eld thought twenty-five feet ought to be added for its top; which makes the whole length of the tree, when growing, two hundred and sixty feet. Others were believed to exceed this, both in height and diameter.

During the time of Mr. Eld's absence, Mr. Colvocoressis remained at the camp, and Mr. Brackenridge made short excursions to the south of the Chickeeles. The country on this side of the river is covered with a thick spruce forest, and the soil appears to differ much from that of the north, being poor, and composed of a mixture of sand and gravel, while on the north side it is an alluvial deposit, averaging from a half to two-thirds of a mile in width, well adapted to yield good crops of grain. From the marks on the trees, however, it is believed to be subject to an annual inundation of considerable depth. The weather continued dry and clear.

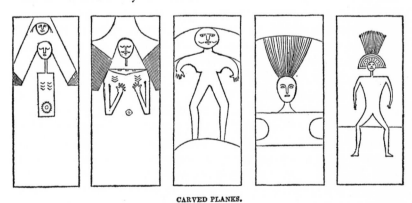

CARVED PLANKS.

Near this encampment were found some rudely carved painted

planks, of which Mr. Eld made a drawing. They are represented in the wood-cut on the opposite page.

These planks were placed upright, and nothing could be learned of their origin. The colours were exceedingly bright, of a kind of red pigment.

In descending the Chickeeles the next morning, they soon perceived by its shores that there was an ebb and flow of the waters. Mr. Eld tried its current, and found it setting flood about one fathom per hour. As they proceeded, the shores lost some of their luxuriance of foliage, the banks had become high, and so muddy that they had some little difficulty in finding a suitable place to encamp. Some talcose slate was seen to compose the bluffs on the south side of the river, but it was so soft and fragile that it could not be brought away. The only natives seen this day were two miserable-looking beings of the Chickeeles tribe, but they could not understand the interpreter Joe, either in the Nisqually or Chinook dialect. The party encamped in a hemlock grove, so thick as to render it impossible for the usual nightly observations to be taken. The surf was distinctly audible from the camp during the night.

On the 31st, after passing two elbows in the river, the cape on the south of the entrance to Gray's Harbour was seen. The flood-tide was very strong against them, so that they made but slow progress, and as they opened out the harbour and entered it, they found a strong southwest wind blowing, which caused a short and disagreeable sea, that very nearly swamped their small canoe, and obliged them to run for the lee shore. Here all the things were taken out and placed to dry, on one of the huge trees that had been brought down by the freshets. From this awkward situation they were relieved by the old squaw chief, who had preceded them from Nisqually. She came over in her large canoe, with ten Indians, and offered to carry the party over to the weather shore, where they could encamp in a less exposed place. The offer was gladly accepted, and they were taken over to the village.

Mr. Eld here endeavoured to treat for the purchase of a large canoe, in which attempt his patience was soon exhausted, for when the bargain was all but closed, difficulties of a trivial nature were brought up which entirely broke off the negotiation. The Indians of this village proved themselves to be in all respects like the tribes in the interior, who will never adhere to a bargain if they can avoid it.

Mr. Eld and his party had now a great many difficulties to contend with in carrying forward a survey of the harbour. These arose as well from the weather as the want of means. The Indians for some days continued unwilling to lend them any aid in the management of their canoes, and none of them could be induced to venture out in what they deemed stormy weather; another reason for not engaging in the service was, they did not wish to leave their wives behind. It being at last agreed that their wives should accompany them, Mr. Colvoco-ressis embarked in order to join Mr. Eld; but to do this it was necessary to encounter both the wind and sea, in consequence of which the Indians refused to proceed unless they had an extra allowance of powder and tobacco.

This being refused, they quietly steered the canoe back to the encampment. On arriving there, it soon became evident to Mr. Col-vocoressis that their intention was to take away their canoe, for they at once began to put in her the few things they possessed. He there-fore took two of their guns, and concealed them in one of the tents. An Indian, the moment Mr. Colvocoressis's back was turned to the tents, drew his knife, rushed into them, and brought forth the guns, one of which he handed to a woman. The musket which the squaw had was again taken, upon which the Indians said that they would complete their bargain, and induced Mr. Colvocoressis to believe they would do so. He therefore embarked, and they proceeded with apparent willing-ness, until they came opposite their own village, where they landed, and refused to go any further. They, however, offered him a small canoe, to take him across the river, and the Indian to whom the musket they had taken belonged, ferried him across. In the evening, the Indians returned to ask for the musket, but it was refused until they should return the axe that had been left in the canoe, and agree to abide by the bargain they had made to render them assistance. The next day the axe was restored, and the musket given up. After this, a more friendly disposition was evinced, as Mr. Eld supposes from the fact of their having learnt from Nisqually who they were.

From the 1st to the 6th of August, the party effected little, and their supply of provisions was becoming very low. On the latter day they shifted their camp, about five miles toward the capes, to a small patch of meadow-land, near one of the small streams which empty into the harbour.

After remaining here a few days, they selected another spot, at the South Head; and on the 10th, the Indians failing to perform their engagements, they moved their articles themselves to their new encampment. They had now very nearly exhausted their provisions, and were living on the dead fish they picked up on the beach (a sort of hake) and some berries. From continual exposure to wet, with hard work, as well as scanty and bad food, they all became very feeble and sick, and were able to do but little work. On the 13th, Lieutenant De Haven, whom I had sent over, arrived, and relieved them; and on his return to Baker's Bay, twenty days' provisions were sent with a party of Kanakas, under the guidance of Boileau, a Canadian.

This supply reached them on the 19th August, from which time they proceeded rapidly with the survey, when the weather would permit. Previous to the arrival of Lieutenant De Haven, Mr. Eld and his party had parted with their own clothing and blankets, for the purpose of effecting the purchase of a large canoe to carry on their work. The Indians refused to deliver it, except for actual pay; for they had not yet learned to value the small pieces of paper, or orders on the Company's store, so much prized in the upper country, and which are there usually preferred to the articles themselves. The threat to stop trading for powder, Mr. Eld found was a strong inducement to accomplish any object with the Indians, for they prize this and tobacco beyond any other articles, always excepting rum.

Mr. Eld, in one instance, treated one of the Indians to a pipe and tobacco, which affected him so much that they thought he was going into a fit, and created considerable alarm. This effect arises from their mode of using the pipe, for they invariably swallow the smoke, and retain the greatest part of it in the stomach and lungs.

On the 24th, the survey was finished, and they prepared for their departure. The tract of land bordering on the Chickeeles, below the mouth of the Sachap, and around Gray's Harbour, is of a poor description for cultivation. The spruce forest extends down to the water's edge, except in a few places around the harbour, where there are patches of salt marsh, which produce course grasses and cat's-tail (Typha). The salt creeks into which the tide flows are generally very tortuous; and the meadows are occasionally overflowed at spring-tides. The only piece of land that appeared suitable for cultivation, was immediately within the South Head; but this is of small extent. The coast, as far as Cape Shoalwater, is no more than a smooth sandy beach, which rises in a gentle acclivity to a line of low sand-hills.

Mr. Brackenridge describes the coast vegetation as consisting of Oberonia, Neottia, Ambrosia, two species of Aster, several Gramineæ, an Armeria, with a number of saline plants; the Gaultheria is found in great abundance, bearing a palatable berry, of which the party had occasion to make use. For further information respecting the plants of this section, I must refer to the Botanical Report.

Gray's Harbour seems to offer but few facilities for commercial purposes. The entrance is narrow, the width being from one-half to

two-thirds of a mile, with dangerous breakers on both sides. The
depth of water is from five to seven fathoms. The space, after entering, is extensive, but the greater part of it is filled up with mud-
flats, which are bare at low water, and confine the harbour suitable
for the anchorage of vessels to very small limits. The river Chickeeles, before entering into the harbour, increases in width to several
hundred feet, and is navigable for vessels drawing twelve feet water,
eight miles above its mouth. The harbour is only suitable for vessels
of from one to two hundred tons; and there are places where such
vessels may find security between the mud shoals, some distance within
the capes.

The tides here are irregular, and influenced by the winds and
weather; the time of high water at full and change was found to be
11^h 30^m.

Fogs prevail very frequently during the summer season. Our party
remained at this place for twenty-three days, three-fourths of which
time it blew a strong gale from either the southwest or northwest,
accompanied with a dense fog, that rendered it impossible to see
farther than half a mile.

The Indians in this portion of the country are not numerous. The
region at the head of Puget Sound is inhabited by a tribe called the
Toandos, whose number Mr. Eld was unable to learn. The Sachals
are about forty in number: they reside about the lake of the same
name, and along the river Chickeeles: they appear to be a kind
and inoffensive tribe. The Sachap tribe numbers about sixty: they
are not as well off for clothing as the former, and few of them were
supplied with fire-arms; they reside on the borders of the Sachap
river. The Chickeeles tribe number from one hundred and fifty to
two hundred, and inhabit the country around Gray's Harbour: their
pricinipal place of abode is on the north point of Gray's Harbour,
which is generally occupied by those passing to and fro, and where
they await fine weather. Mr. Eld found this tribe supplied with good
muskets, blankets, and knives: they paint their faces, and have altogether a warlike appearance. At one time during the stay of the
party they were disposed to be troublesome, but the men being constantly on the watch, to protect themselves, remained unmolested,
though occasionally annoyed at the disposition evinced to take advantage of any oversight. The chief of this tribe is spoken of by the
party in very high terms, for his kindness to them. He seemed
mortified at the events which occurred, and took much pains to keep
his people in order. In this, notwithstanding he possessed little au-

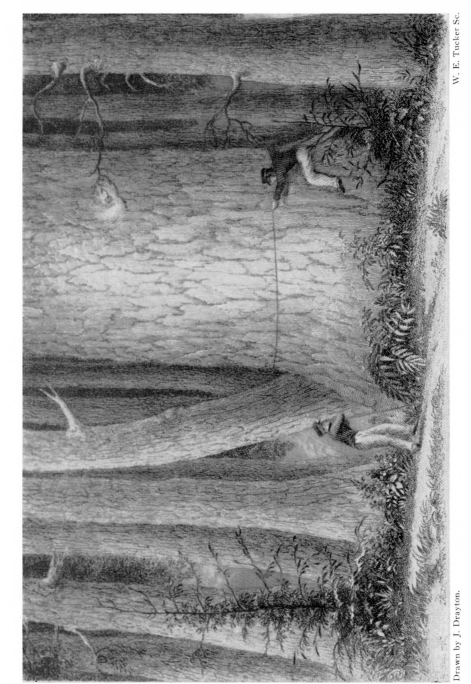

Drawn by J. Drayton.

W. E. Tucker Sc.

PINE FOREST, OREGON.

thority among his tribe, he succeeded, although with difficulty. As a proof of his good intentions, he invariably returned all the signals the others had stolen.

This tribe lives principally on salmon, which they take during the season in vast quantities, and the fish are said to be as fine as those taken in the Columbia. On the Chickeeles, and in its branches, are many of the weirs and stakes that have been already described. Sturgeon are also taken in great numbers, and of a superior quality.

It may be inferred from their seldom receiving any supplies of venison through the Indians, or meeting with any themselves, that there is but little game in this part of the country.

They shot a few grouse, some wild geese were seen, and the mud-flats were covered with white gulls in immense numbers, among which were a few pelicans.

The amusements of the Indians, and the manner of lounging away their time, were similar to those of the other tribes before spoken of.

On the 24th, they were glad to leave Gray's Harbour, after having, by great perseverance and with much fatigue, completed the survey. Mr. Eld now took up the remaining portion of the work he was ordered to perform, namely, to trace the coast to Cape Disappointment. The Indians whom he hired to take the canoe around by water, preferred to pass close along the beach, inside the surf, by tracking the canoe: notwithstanding there was a very heavy surf, they managed to pass along very quickly. This is the mode they always adopt in journeying along the coast with their canoes, to avoid accident from the heavy surf, of which they have much dread. The evening of the day on which they left Gray's Harbour, they reached a small islet, distant fifteen miles from Cape Shoalwater, where they found the lodge of the Chickeeles chief before spoken of, who supplied them with dried salmon, &c.

The coast between Gray's Harbour and Cape Shoalwater is bordered by sand-hills, behind which, from the Indians' account, there are lakes and streams of fresh water, in which plenty of beaver are found.

From this chief they hired another canoe, and accompanied by him they proceeded through Shoalwater Bay towards Cape Disappointment. The two canoes separated, which caused them to pass over the two portages between Shoalwater and Baker's Bay: that to the east is about four and a half miles in length, while that to the west is six or seven miles across. The former is usually preferred by the Indians, and is one of the main passes of communication between the different tribes on the sea-coast. The woods through which they passed were of spruce trees, some of which were of large dimensions; the lesser plants were principally Vaccinium, Ledums, and some candleberry-bushes (Myrica).

On the 27th they reached the Flying-Fish, then in Baker's Bay, and were taken over to Astoria.

Mr. Eld received, on his arrival at Astoria, my orders to repair with his party to Vancouver; where, being furnished by Mr. Birnie with a large flat-bottomed barge, he set out to join me at that place, which he reached on the 31st August.

I cannot refrain from expressing the satisfaction I felt at the manner in which the service was performed, and deem it my duty to make known to the country the commendable perseverance with which this party persisted in completing the duty assigned them, regardless of inconvenience, privation, and discomfort. This tour forms a part of the operations of the Expedition that I look back upon with pride and pleasure, and I feel that my thanks are especially due to Passed Midshipmen Eld and Colvocoressis, and Mr. Brackenridge, for their devotion to the service in which they were engaged.

Orders were immediately given for them to join the over-land expedition to California, under Lieutenant Emmons, who was just about proceeding to the Willamette Valley, where his party had been organized, with our own force and the settlers and trappers who were engaged to accompany it to California. After the party was collected, it consisted of—

Lieutenant Emmons,	T. R. Peale, Naturalist,
Passed Midshipman Eld,	W. Rich, Botanist,
Passed Midshipman Colvocoressis,	J. D. Dana, Geologist,
Assistant-Surgeon Whittle,	A. T. Agate, Artist,
Doughty, Seaman,	J. D. Brackenridge, Assistant Botanist,
Sutton, "	Baptist Guardipii, Guide,
Waltham, "	Tibbats,
Merzer, "	Black,
Sergeant Stearns,	Warfields,
Corporal Hughes,	Wood,
Private Marsh,	Molair,
Private Smith,	Inass.

Those who joined the party for a safe escort, were Mr. Walker and family, consisting of his wife, sister, three sons, and two daughters; Burrows, wife, and child; Nichols, with Warfields' wife and child.

The whole party numbered thirty-nine, with seventy-six animals, forty-four of which were private property.

Lieutenant Emmons at first found much difficulty in organizing his party, on account of having to deal with persons who had little

or no regard for the promises they made, or the engagements they entered into. This feature of character proceeds both from a desire to obtain more money, and a want of stability of purpose. Many difficulties were encountered by him in consequence of the change of his route to California, which many of those who were to have accompanied him were unwilling to undertake. These were the very best men we had engaged. Every kind of embarrassment seemed to come upon him at once: delays and disappointments occurred every day; sickness overtook the party; rumours were circulated of danger from the Indians, who it was said were determined to oppose the party and cut it off. Some of the settlers refused to re-engage, because their crops required attention, and their harvest might be lost; others said that they could not leave their families for so long a time; and amidst these various sources of delay, the animals strayed away, or were carried off. The whole, finally, resolved itself into a demand for higher wages.

Lieutenant Emmons, though exceedingly annoyed by all these difficulties, showed himself fully equal to them, and by patience and perseverance overcame them all. Mr. Rodgers, whom I had designated as the provider of the party, and in whom I was told great reliance could be placed, was not exactly suited to such a task, being connected more or less with the inhabitants of the valley, and about to become one of the residents; he also was soon unable to attend to business on account of sickness: before the organization of the second party, therefore, he was discharged and paid off. At this point I shall leave the narrative of the operations of the over-land party, until I come down to the date when they again joined me at San Francisco.

The observations and surveys in the neighbourhood of Vancouver being finished, we prepared for our departure. The weather during our stay had been delightful, and we enjoyed ourselves very much in the company of Dr. M'Laughlin, Mr. Douglass, and the officers of the Hudson Bay Company.

I have before spoken of their attentions, but I feel that my expressions are few in comparison with the numerous kindnesses we all received. Even Billy Bruce the gardener made us his debtor, by sending us repeatedly some of the fine fruit and vegetables grown under his care. I have endeavoured to repay him, by sending him seeds; but the route is so long and circuitous, that it is questionable whether they ever arrive, and when they come to hand, if I shall not be classed by him with those who have sent "trash" to Vancouver, for him to waste his time and experience on, in attempting to cultivate.

Among the officers of the Hudson Bay Company, I must not forget to mention Dr. Barclay, whose kind attentions in procuring specimens for the Expedition, entitle him to our gratitude.

Sir George Simpson stayed only a few days. He took his departture under a salute of guns from the Cadborough, and the attendance of all the officers and dependants of the forts. Mr. Douglass went with him; and in his suite was also Mr. Von Freeman, a Russian gentleman, with whom I was much pleased. He was going to Sitka, and I believe was one of the officers of the Russian Company.

The number of posts occupied by the Hudson Bay Company in this territory is twenty-five: these are located at the best points for trade, and so as to secure the resort of the Indians, without interfering with their usual habits. Places are also occupied in the vicinity of their abodes during the most favourable part of the year, for obtaining the proceeds of their hunting. This is regulated with much skill: and the portion of the country once under their care is never suffered to become exhausted of furs; for, whenever they discover a decrease, the ground is abandoned for several years, until the animals have time to increase again.

A charge has been made against the Company, that they were desirous of exterminating the beaver south of the Columbia, and would continue to hunt them until every fur-bearing animal was exhausted. This, from the information I received, I believe to be erroneous; the story has probably proceeded from feelings of rivalry on the part of those who spread the report.

Another charge made against them, of exciting attacks on the free trappers, who are generally from our borders, is to be received with many allowances. It has been made in many cases from interested motives; and I am satisfied that nothing of this kind could emanate from Vancouver, or from any of the officers.

The whole conduct of Dr. M'Laughlin is totally at variance with such a course: every facility has been at all times extended to newcomers and settlers; it is sufficient that they are of good character, and the use of cattle, horses, farming utensils, and supplies, is invariably extended to facilitate their operations, until such time as they are able to provide for themselves.

During our stay at Vancouver, I had the pleasure of seeing many members of the Willamette Mission; but they were unable to give me much information. They invariably spoke of Dr. M'Laughlin in the highest terms: they were averse to his absolute rule over the whole territory, and, although it was considered by them as despotic, they could not adduce any instance of the wrong application of his power. He is notwithstanding extremely unpopular among all classes of our countrymen, but for what reason it is difficult to conceive.

Dr. M'Laughlin obligingly favoured me with the heights of the stopping-places, or encampments, on the route that is usually taken by their parties crossing the Rocky Mountains: the results were obtained by the boiling point of water. The journey was made during the months of August, September, and October, 1839.

			WATER BOILS.	HEIGHT DEDUCED.
August 29th,	at Edmonton, ...		207°	2566 feet.
September 22d,	" Jasper's House, . . .		204·5	3867
" 29th,	" Camp d'Origal, . . .		203·5	4391
" 30th,	" Camp de Fusil, . . .		201	5716
" "	" Punchbowl, ...		198	7324
" "	" Head of Grand Cote, . .		202	5188
October 1st,	" Bottom of Grand Cote, .		204	4131
" 3d,	" Boat Encampment, . .		205	3607
" 8th,	" Colville, ...		208	2049
" 14th,	" Wallawalla, ...		209·5	1286

This may be considered as a near approximation to the true height, and at several of the places where the barometer has been also used, there is a very close coincidence in the results.

The instrument used for the experiment was one of Newman's make, and exceedingly convenient for such purposes, offering great facility in use, without the danger of accident from its size.

The trade and operations of the Hudson Bay Company are extensive, and the expense with which they are attended is very great. I am inclined to think that it is hardly possible for any one to form an exact estimate of the amount of profit they derive from their business on the west side of the mountains. The stock of the Company certainly pays a large dividend; and it is asserted that in addition a very considerable surplus has been accumulated to meet any emergency; yet it may be questioned whether their trade in the Oregon Territory yields any profit, although it is now conducted at much less cost than formerly. This dimunition of cost arises from the fact that a great part of the provisions are now raised in the country by the labour of their own servants.

The Puget Sound Company, although it has been in operation for several years, has made no dividends. The accumulation of their live-stock may, however, be considered as an equivalent for moneyed profits. In the event, however, of the country becoming the abode of a civilized community, the farms and other land possessed by this Company must become very valuable, as the posts occupy all the points most favourably situated for trade, and the agricultural establishments, have been placed in many of the best positions for farming operations.   The utmost economy is practised in every part of the establishment of the Hudson Bay Company, and great exertions are made to push their operations over a larger field of action.   Mercantile houses, supported by the credit and capital of the Company, have even been established at the Sandwich Islands and San Francisco, where articles of every description imported in the vessels of the Company may be purchased.

The value of all the furs obtained on this coast does not exceed forty thousand pounds annually; and when the cost of keeping up their posts, and a marine composed of four ships and a steamer, is taken into account, and allowances made for losses, interest, and insurance, little surplus can be left for distribution. I am, indeed, persuaded, that the proceeds of their business will not long exceed their expenses, even if they do so at present.   The statement of the Company's affairs presents no criterion by which to judge the success of their business on the Northwest Coast.   I learned that it was the general impression among the officers, that such has been the falling off in the trade, that it does not now much more than pay expenses.

On my first visit to Vancouver, Dr. M'Laughlin was kind enough to offer to keep a meteorological diary for me, during my stay on the coast, that I might have the means of comparison.   They had formerly been in the habit of noting the changes that occurred, and for many years had kept a journal; but this had been for some years omitted. The task would be but trifling in such a well-regulated establishment, and it is surprising that it should not have claimed more attention. The night observations seem to be the principal difficulty.   In the register kept during our stay, the instruments were only noted in the daytime, and the record is not available for the mean temperature of the twenty-four hours; but as it may serve to show the state of the weather, during the summer months, at Vancouver, I will give an abstract from it.   The barometer and thermometer were both compared with our standard, and found nearly to coincide.

MONTHS.	6 A. M.		2 P. M.		6 P. M.	
	BAROM.	THERMOM.	BAROM.	THERMOM.	BAROM.	THERMOM.
June . . .	30·71 in.	51°	30·27 in.	63°	30·30 in.	62°
July. . . .	30·40	61	30·36	87	30·37	72
August. . .	30·28	60	30·27	86	30·29	70
September. .	30·28	53	30·25	78	30·30	58

This gives the mean standing of the barometer and thermometer, during the day hours, at 30·32 in., and 66·33° for the summer months.

The state of the weather, during the period of one hundred and six days, was as follows:

Fair,	. . . . .	76 days.
Cloudy,	. . . . .	19 "
Rain,	. . . . .	11 "
		106

In my inquiries of the residents, I am inclined to the opinion that the above is a very fair estimate of the weather, though they almost all differed in their statements: some spoke of the season as a very bad one, others thought it was very fine. The crops of all descriptions of grain were good, which I supposed to be the best criterion.

The climate of the western section, throughout the year, is mild; and they neither experience extreme heat in summer, nor severe cold in winter. I am disposed to believe this to be owing to the constant prevalence of the southwesterly or ocean winds. It certainly is not owing to the influence of any warm stream setting along its shores. The current near the coast sets to the southeast, and is of a cold temperature: it would rather tend to lessen the heats in summer than the cold in winter. There have been no observations kept by the missionaries in this lower section of the country. It is liable, from the experience of our parties, to early frosts, owing to the proximity of the Snowy Mountains. Frosts sometimes occur in the latter part of August, which check all vegetation at that early season.

The southwest winds are caused by the vast extent of the sandy and arid country lying east of the Cascade and Californian range of mountains, which becoming heated rarefies the air, and causes an indraught from the west. This current is found to increase in violence as the rarefied region is approached; and so constant is this draught, that we experienced only three days of easterly winds during our stay, and these were very moderate in force. Immediately on the coast, the winds are from the west-southwest to west-northwest: these maintain their direction until they reach the interior, and blow with great violence.

The winters are invariably what would be termed open ones with us. Snow seldom falls, and when it does, it rarely lasts more than two or three days. The rains during this season are frequent, though not violent. The climate in the western section, from all accounts, is not unlike that of England, and would be termed a wet one. The winter of 1840 was the severest they had yet experienced.

The middle section is, on the contrary, exceedingly dry, and the temperature more changeable, the variations being great and sudden. The mercury has been known to fall as low as —18° in the winter, and to rise as high as 108° in the shade, in summer. In Appendix XIII., Vol. IV., will be found a register of the temperature, kept at one of the missionary stations, Lapwai, on the Kooskooskee. It may be said to be on the eastern border of the middle section.

The eastern section has an exceedingly variable climate: it fluctuates from cold to hot in a few hours, ranging from fifty or sixty degrees of temperature; yet, from the accounts I have, from very respectable authority, the cold is by no means severe for any length of time. The Rev. Mr. Smith, who was two years there, assured me that the cattle and horses required no food than what they could pick up, the natural hay before spoken of being sufficient for their support.

The climate throughout Oregon is thought to be salubrious for the white race; and was considered so by the Indians, prior to the year 1830, when the ague and fever, or any disease resembling it, was not known to exist. The Indians fully believe, to this day, that Captain Dominis introduced the disease in 1830. Since that time, it has committed frightful ravages among them; not so much, perhaps, from the violence of the disease itself, as the manner in which they treat it. It was not until quite lately that they were willing to be treated after our mode, and they still in many cases prefer the incantations and practices of the medicine-man.

I satisfied myself that the accounts given of the depopulation of this country are not exaggerated; for places were pointed out to me where dwelt whole tribes, that have been entirely swept off; and, during the time of the greatest mortality, the shores of the river were strewed with the dead and dying. This disease occurs, it is said, semi-annually, and in the case of foreigners, it is more mild at each succeeding attack.

Owing to the above causes, the population is much less than I expected to find it. I made every exertion to obtain correct information, and believe that at the time of our visit, the following was very nearly the truth, viz.:

Vancouver and Washington Island, ...	5,000
From latitude 50° to 54° N, on the main, ...	2,000
Penn's Cove, Whidby's Island, including the main land (Sachet tribe), ...	650
Hood's Canal (Suquamish and Toando tribes), . . .	500
Birch Bay, ...	300
Fraser's River, ...	500
	8,950

Brought forward, ...	8,950
Clalams at Port Discovery, New Dungeness, . . .	350
Port Townsend, ...	70
Claset tribe, Cape Flattery and Point Grenville, . . .	1,250
Nisqually, ...	200
Chickeeles and Puget Sound, ...	700
Port Orchard, ...	150
Cowlitz, ...	330
Okonagan, ...	300
Colville and Spokane, ...	450
Kilamukes, ...	400
Chinooks, ...	209
Clatsops, ...	220
Cascades, ...	150
Pillar Rock, Oak Point, and Columbia River, . . .	300
Willamette Falls and Valley, ...	275
Dalles, ...	250
De Chute's and John Day's River, ...	300
Yakima, ...	100
Wallawalla, ...	1,100
Blackfeet, that dwell principally on the west side of the	
Rocky Mountains, ...	1,000
Umpquas, ...	400
Rogues' River, ...	500
Klamets, ...	300
Shaste, ...	500
Callapuyas, ...	600
Total, .	19,354

The whole territory may, therefore, be considered as containing about twenty thousand Indians; and this, from a careful revision of the data obtained by myself and some of the officers, I am satisfied, is rather above than under the truth. The whites and half-breeds were between seven and eight hundred. One hundred and fifty were Americans. The number of the latter has, however, increased very much since the year 1840, as many emigrants have crossed the mountains. The decrease of the red race is, no doubt, equivalent to the increase by immigration.

The surveying parties having returned, on the 14th we took leave of Vancouver. After proceeding down to the mouth of the Willamette, we anchored, for the purpose of finishing the soundings and making an examination of the channels into which the river is here divided by a few islands.

This work being completed, we dropped down several miles, to overtake the sounding parties. Here we were a good deal annoyed from the burning of the prairies by the Indians, which filled the atmosphere with a dense smoke, and gave the sun the appearance of being viewed through a smoked glass. We were, fortunately, in a great degree, independent of it, as it was not necessary to see more than a short distance to discover the signals for the soundings. It however prevented me from verifying my astronomical stations, which I was desirous of doing.

Acting-Master Sinclair, who had been despatched to Vancouver for some articles belonging to the Oregon, that had been left there, joined us below Warrior's Point, on the 19th, with letters and news that had been brought from the United States by an over-land party. These letters were very acceptable, as we had not received any advices from home for twenty-two months, and tended to revive our spirits, as well as encourage our exertions. On the 20th, we anchored again off Coffin Rock, near which we found a depth of twenty-five fathoms, which is the deepest water within the capes. This place is sixty miles from the mouth of the river, and eight miles above the confluence of the Cowlitz. The shores here are composed of trap and a conglomerate, the last of which is the same rock as that which occurs below, and has already been spoken of. The Coffin Rock, which is not more than sixty feet in diameter, and twelve feet above the water, appears to have been exclusively reserved for the burial of chiefs. Dr. Holmes procured here some fine specimens of Flathead skulls for our collection. We anchored the same evening off the Cowlitz.

Early the next morning, I proceeded up the Cowlitz in my gig, in order to finish the survey of that stream and examine the strata of coal said to exist there. After entering it, it was with difficulty that I recognized the river; for there is a greater difference than even in the Columbia, between its high and low states. After passing up the Cowlitz several miles, I encountered rapids, through which it was necessary to drag the boat by line. I found, after great exertion and fatigue, we could not ascend beyond thirteen miles; for it had become so shallow that the boat would not float, and we had not strength enough to force her over the wide bars of gravel and sand, that had apparently accumulated during the last spring. After securing some specimens of lignite that were found embedded in the alluvial banks, and taking observations for time, I turned back; and feeling anxious to reach the brig at an early hour, I ventured to shoot one of the rapids. In doing this, we all had a narrow escape; and particularly two of the boat's crew, who were in great danger of their lives. We fortunately escaped, but with considerable damage to the boat and a few bruises, the whole of which was the work of an instant. This taught me not to venture upon such an experiment again, and I felt thankful to escape as we did. The Cowlitz is not navigable, except at high water during the spring and fall; and even then it is difficult to ascend, on account of the strength of its current.

We had now overtaken the sounding parties, and, aided by the boats of the brig, were enabled to push the work towards a close. Having reached the influence of the tide below Oak Point, all fears of the ague and fever vanished: we had indeed been extremely fortunate in exemption from this disease, and only those suffered from its attacks who had been before exposed. Those affected belonged chiefly to the Peacock, and the larger portion were Sandwich Islanders. The crew of the Porpoise were generally exempt from it: all recovered from the slight attacks under a simple treatment. I felt not a little satisfaction at disappointing the knowing ones, who had prognosticated the certainty of my having all hands sick and dying by attempting the survey in the unhealthy season. When we reached Astoria, we had nearly all hands on duty.

On the 26th, we had again reach Katalamet Point, the lower end of Puget Island. The brig passed down the usual channel on the south side, while I surveyed the northern passage. The latter is about four miles in length.

Puget Island affords no land fit for cultivation, and during the season of freshets is overflowed. It is fringed around its borders with cottonwood, willow, pine, and hazel, &c.; but it may be considered valueless.

At this anchorage I was joined by Michel La Framboise, who brought a supply of fresh beef for the crew, which they were in much need of. Since I had first seen Michel, I had learned more of his history and the cause which led him to complain of a want of advancement. I regret to say, that, like too many others, he ought to look to himself as the cause of his misfortune, instead of indulging in complaints.

He confirmed much of the information I had received, and gave me full statements of the population, which I found to agree with what he had already imparted to officers belonging to the Company, as well as the Expedition.

I questioned him relative to the stories respecting the shooting of Indians, on the route to and from California, and he told me they had no battles, but said it was necessary to keep them always at a distance. On my repeating the question, whether the reports we had heard of several being killed during the late expedition were true, he, Frenchman-like, shrugged his shoulders and answered: "Ah, monsieur, ils sont des mauvaises gens: il faut en prendre garde et tirer sur eux quelquefois."

On the 29th of September we again reached the Pillar Rock, and on the 3d of October we passed through the Tongue Point Channel. Before doing this, we took the precaution to buoy it out, and then towed the vessels through at high water. This enabled me to lay down its tortuous course with accuracy, although I was aware that there is little probability of its remaining over the season without some material change. The new and direct channel discovered by us, leading up from Tongue Point, will supersede the necessity of using it, and from its direct course, is more likely to be permanent; but the channels in this river will be always more or less subject to change, from the impediments the large trees drifting down cause, when they ground on the shoals.

The same evening we anchored about two miles above Astoria, and in order to lose no time, I proceeded there in my boat to make arrangements for getting off the stores, and embarking every thing previous to our departure.

I found that Purser Speiden had prepared for us ten thousand pounds of the best bread we had had during the cruise: this had been accomplished by his great perseverance and attention to the business, and I was thus relieved from all anxiety in regard to that indispensable article of the ration.

On the 1st of October, the Porpoise anchored at Astoria, and every body was now engaged in expediting the embarkation of stores on board of both vessels; the officers were detailed temporarily to the Oregon, whilst the necessary observations for the chronometers and magnetism were again made.

It now became important that the two larger vessels should be got to sea as early as possible. I therefore determined to seize the first opportunity that should offer for crossing the bar, and to return myself in the tender to complete the survey. We, in consequence, proceeded on the 2d to Baker's Bay, whilst the boats were still employed under Lieutenant De Haven in taking soundings. Acting-Master Knox and Passed Midshipman Reynolds, were now ordered to the Porpoise and Oregon, for the purpose of piloting them to sea, when an opportunity should serve. In Baker's Bay we found the Company's schooner, the Cadborough, which had been waiting three weeks for an opportunity to get over the bar.

As the Peacock's launch could not be taken with us, I had at one time an intention of sending her along the coast to San Francisco. The weather and advanced state of the season, however, would have rendered such a voyage dangerous; I therefore came to the determination of providing her with every essential to fit her to be used as a pilot-boat in the mouth of the river, or for the relief of vessels in distress. Mr. Birnie, on my asking him to take charge of her for that object, would have readily consented to do so for the Company, but had no authority. I therefore immediately wrote to Dr. M'Laughlin, to say that I had placed the launch at his disposal, and to request that she might be put under the supervision of the Company's officers, for the above purposes. She was completely fitted, and delivered over to Mr. Birnie. The letters to Dr. M'Laughlin on this subject will be found in Appendix V. In consequence of my departure from the coast, I received no answer from him, but have understood from other sources that the boat had been taken charge of. Her construction was admirably adapted for that purpose, and I am sure that if any disaster should occur, the assistance she will render will be of great benefit.

On the 5th, the prospect of passing the bar was favourable, and at 2^h 30^m P. M. the Company's bark Columbia, which had been lying off and on for the last week, entered. On passing the vessels she saluted us, and proceeded up the river to Astoria. At 3^h 30^m, I determined on making the attempt to get to sea. We quickly got the vessels under way, and in an hour afterwards we had passed the bar in safety.

The Cadborough followed our example, and went to sea also. Her master, before we got under way, had strong misgivings as to undertaking the risk at so late an hour both of the day and tide. The vessels of the Hudson Bay Company never attempt to pass either in or out, unless the opportunity is such as will warrant the master in making the attempt. They consider that there is sufficient risk at the best of times, and are unwilling to increase it. I have already stated that the entrance to the Columbia is impracticable for two-thirds of the year. This arises from the fact that it can never be entered at night, and in the day only at particular times of the tide and direction of the wind. Unlike all known ports, it requires both the tide and wind to be contrary, to insure any degree of safety. Those who may desire to be farther informed on this subject, are referred to the Hydrographical Memoir of the cruise.

Having succeeded in getting the brigs beyond the risk of detention, I gave them orders to await my return, and went on board the tender, to pass again into the river, for the purpose of completing all that remained of the survey. The Company's bark Columbia had just returned from the northern posts. The master, Mr. Broughton, was kind enough to give me much information respecting the northern coasts, and the Indian tribes: he likewise presented the Expedition with many curiosities of native workmanship, some of which showed much ingenuity, particularly their pipes and masks. The latter are used in their theatrical exhibitions, which are represented by those who have witnessed them, as affording them much entertainment, and a pastime in which they very frequently indulge; many of these masks are represented with the spoon-lip. As this ornament belongs to the female sex, they also

MASKS OF THE NORTHWEST INDIANS.

engage in the diversion. Some of the masks are sufficiently hideous, while others are carved with skill: they use the soft pine for this pur-
pose. The wood is variously stained with red, black, and yellow marks. The two of these represented in the engraving will give a good idea of those that are the best executed. The pipes, saucers, &c., are usually carved from clay.

PIPES OF THE NORTHWEST INDIANS.

The survey we finished by the morning of the 10th October, when we again reached Baker's Bay, and being determined to lose no time, we made the attempt to pass the bar: though we succeeded in doing so, I am satisfied it was at great risk; for, as I have been told is frequently the case, the wind failed us just at the most critical point, and rendered it doubtful if we should pass. Our situation was dangerous, and a vessel of any other class must have been wrecked. For at least twenty minutes I was in doubt whether we could effect our object; but by the use of sweeps we accomplished it, principally through the exertions of the extra men, belonging to the surveying boats, whom we had on board.

The Oregon was the only vessel in sight; and when I boarded her, I learned that they had not seen the Porpoise for three days. The next day she hove in sight, and the arrangements were soon completed.

I now supplied the tender with water and other requisites, and gave Mr. Knox orders to take a few more soundings on the outside of the bar, and then proceed along the coast as far as latitude 42° N., and to examine it, and the mouth of the Umpqua.

Previous to leaving the Columbia river, I addressed the following letter to Dr. M'Laughlin and Mr. Douglass.

U. S. Brig Porpoise,
Baker's Bay,
October 5th, 1841.

GENTLEMEN,—

My last duty, before leaving the Columbia, I feel to be that of expressing to you my sincere thanks for the important aid and facilities which you have afforded the Expedition on all occasions, for carrying out the object of our visit to this part of the world; and be assured it will prove a very pleasing part of my duty to make a due representation of it to my government.

Your personal kindness and friendly attentions to myself and officers, from our first arrival, and also to Captain Hudson and his officers after the wreck of the Peacock, have laid me under many obligations, which I trust it may be at some future day in our power to return.

We all would request through you an expression of your feelings for the many attentions and kindnesses received, and the pleasures afforded us by the officers of the Hudson Bay Company's service, with whom we have had any intercourse, which will be long remembered with pleasure.

With my sincere wishes for the health, happiness, and prosperity of yourselves and families, I am, very truly,

Your obedient servant,
CHARLES WILKES,
Commanding Exploring Expedition.

To JOHN M'LAUGHLIN and
JAMES DOUGLASS, ESQUIRES,
Chief Factors, H. B. C. Service, Vancouver.

At the same time, I wrote a letter to our government, informing them of the assistance we had received, stating the services these gentlemen had rendered us, and asking that an expression of acknowledgment might be made, through the British minister at Washington, to the Directors of the Hudson Bay Company in England.

On the night of the 15th, we parted company with the Oregon, and did not see her again until she arrived at San Francisco. We coasted along to the southward, in the Porpoise. The land is high and mountainous, and may be seen at a great distance. Soundings of dark sand are obtained, in from thirty to forty fathoms water, about fifteen or twenty miles from the land.

The coast south of the Columbia river I regretted we had not an opportunity more particularly to examine: the attempt of the Flying-Fish was unsuccessful; the season had advanced so far as to make it next to impossible to accomplish it in the manner I desired. I have no reason to doubt the correctness of the examinations that have been already made. No ports exist along any part of it, that are accessible to any class of vessels, even those of but very small draught of water; and the impediment that the constant and heavy surf offers, along the whole coast, to a landing in boats, makes this part of our territory comparatively valueless in a commercial point of view. Along a great part of it is an iron-bound shore, rising precipitately from the water. Anchorage in a few places may be had, but only in fair weather, and during the fine season. For a more particular description of the coast, I refer to the Hydrographical Memoir.

On the 18th, we made Cape de los Reyes and the Farallones. In the afternoon we were boarded by a boat from the Company's bark, Cowlitz, in which was her master, Mr. Brochier, and M. Duplot de Mofras. The latter informed me that he had just made a tour through Mexico and California, and was now going to the Columbia, for a passage to Oahu. The same evening, finding that I could not reach the port, I anchored in thirteen fathoms water.

On the 19th, we were under way as soon as the tide made, and at 3 P. M. we anchored near the Vincennes, in Sausalito Bay, on the north side of the entrance. I was gratified to find all well. Lieutenant-Commandant Ringgold reported to me that he had fulfilled the instructions relative to the Sacramento river. Nothing had yet been heard of Lieutenant Emmons; and the next day I despatched the launch up the river to meet his party. The Oregon came in during the afternoon, and I forthwith made such disposition of the officers and men, as I deemed the future wants of the service would require; this, and the operations of the Vincennes, will form the subject of the next chapter.

HATS, NORTHWEST COAST.

CHAPTER II.

CONTENTS.

●

CHAPTER II.

CALIFORNIA.

1841.

fter Lieutenant-Commandant Ringgold joined the Vincennes, she bore away for San Francisco, for the purpose of carrying into effect my instructions (see Appendix VI). She arrived at that port on the 14th of August, and anchored off Yerba Buena. Several vessels, amongst them two Americans, were found here, and intelligence was received of the death of General Harrison, President of the United States.

As soon as the ship anchored, an officer was despatched on shore to call upon the authorities; but none of any description were to be found. The only magistrate, an alcalde, was absent. The frequency of revolutions in this country had caused a great change since the visit of Captain Beechey.

On the 17th, after consultation with the captain of the port, a Mr. Richardson, the ship was moved to the north shore, at Sausalito, or Whaler's Harbour. Water, which it was impossible to obtain at Yerba Buena, on account of the drought that had prevailed for several months, is here to be had from a small spring. After the ship was moored, the boats were hoisted out, and fitted for surveying duties up the river Sacramento.

On approaching the coast in the neighbourhood of San Francisco, the country has by no means an inviting aspect. To the north, it rises in a lofty range, whose highest point is known as the Table Hill, and forms an iron-bound coast from Punto de los Reyes to the mouth of the harbour.

To the south, there is an extended sandy beach, behind which rise the sand-hills of San Bruno, to a moderate height. There are no symptoms of cultivation, nor is the land on either side fit for it; for in the former direction it is mountainous, in the latter sandy, and in both barren. The entrance to the harbour is striking: bold and rocky shores confine the rush of the tide, which bore us on and through a narrow passage into a large estuary: in this, several islands and rocks lie scattered around: some of the islands are clothed with vegetation to their very tops; others are barren and covered with guano, having an immense number of sea-fowls hovering over, around and alighting upon them. The distant shores of the bay extend north and south far beyond the visible horizon, exhibiting one of the most spacious, and at the same time safest ports in the world. To the east rises a lofty inland range, known by the name of La Sierra, brilliant with all the beautiful tints that the atmosphere in this climate produces.

Yerba Buena is the usual though by no means the best anchorage. The town, as is stated, is not calculated to produce a favourable impression on a stranger. Its buildings may be counted, and consist of a large frame building, occupied by the agent of the Hudson Bay Company, a store, kept by Mr. Spears, an American, a billiard-room and bar, a poop cabin of a ship, occupied as a dwelling by Captain Hinckley, a blacksmith's shop, and some out-buildings. These, though few in number, are also far between. With these, I must not forget to enumerate an old dilapidated adobe building, which has a conspicuous position on the top of the hill overlooking the anchorage. When to this we add a sterile soil and hills of bare rock, it will be seen that Yerba Buena and the country around it are any thing but beautiful. This description holds good when the tide is high, but at low water it has for a foreground an extensive mud-flat, which does not add to the beauty of the view.

Although I was prepared for anarchy and confusion, I was surprised when I found a total absence of all government in California, and even its forms and ceremonies thrown aside.

After passing through the entrance, we were scarcely able to distinguish the Presidio; and had it not been for its solitary flag-staff, we could not have ascertained its situation. From this staff no flag floated; the building was deserted, the walls had fallen to decay, the guns were dismounted, and every thing around it lay in quiet. We were not even saluted by the stentorian lungs of some soldier, so customary in Spanish places, even after all political power as well as military and civil rule has fled. I afterwards learned that the Presidio was still a garrison in name, and that it had not been wholly abandoned; but the remnant of the troops stationed there consisted of no more than an officer and one soldier. I was not able to learn the rank of the former, as he was absent, and appeared, at least among the foreigners, to be little known.

At Yerba Buena there was a similar absence of all authority. The only officer was the alcalde, who dwells at the mission of Nostra Señora de los Dolores, some three miles off. He was full of self-importance, making up for what he wanted in the eyes of others by a high estimate of his own dignity. I could find no one who could furnish me with his name, which must be my apology for not recording it in this place. Some excuse may be offered for his inattention to his duties, as I understood that he had just been united in wedlock to a lady of one of the distinguished families of the country; and after such an event in California much gaiety and rejoicing usually follow, until the hilarity at times becomes so uproarious as to end in fighting and bloodshed.

Under the Palermo Mountains, or Table Hill of Beechey, which is two thousand five hundred feet high, and sparsely wooded with a few gnarled and scraggy oaks, the hills open towards the bay into a kind of vale, which had been chosen for the position of the observatory, and where the instruments had been set up under the direction of Lieutenant Carr. This place is well adapted for the resort of whalers. Here they may repair their boats, obtain water, and refit; and from their frequent resort to it, has obtained the name of Whaler's Harbour. The cove is a safe anchorage, being protected from the northwest and westerly winds, which prevail during the summer season, and often blow with great violence.

At the time of our visit, the country altogether presented rather a singular appearance, owing, as I afterwards observed, to the withered vegetation and the ripened wild oats of the country. Instead of a lively green hue, it had generally a tint of a light straw-colour, showing an extreme want of moisture. The drought had continued for eleven months; the cattle were dying in the fields; and the first view of California was not calculated to make a favourable impression either of its beauty or fertility.

I found it very difficult to obtain accurate information in relation to Upper California. The country, at the time of our visit, and for several years previous, had been in a state of revolution; and, as is often the case under similar circumstances, was involved in anarchy and confusion, without laws or security of person and property. It is undergoing such frequent changes, that it is difficult to understand or to describe them.

With California is associated the idea of a fine climate, and a rich and productive soil. This, at least, was the idea with which I entered its far-famed port; but I soon found, from the reports of the officers, after the trial they had had of it during the months of August and September, that their experience altogether contradicted the received opinion upon the first mentioned point. Many of them compared its climate to that of Orange Harbour, at Cape Horn, with its cold bluster-ing winds and cloudy skies. This kind of weather prevails during the greater part of the year, and the comparison is literally true in relation to one portion of California—the sea-coast.

There is, perhaps no other country where there is such a diversity of features, soil, and climate, as California. The surface exhibits the varieties of lofty ranges of mountains, confined valleys, and extensive plains. On the coast, a range of high land extends in length from Cape Mendocino to latitude 32° N., and in breadth into the interior from ten to twenty miles.

The valley of San Juan, of no great extent, lies between these hills and the Sierra, which is a low range of mountains. East of the Sierra is the broad valley of the Sacramento, which is prolonged to the south in that of Buena Ventura, as far as Mount San Bernardino, under the thirty-fourth parallel. Beyond this valley is the California Range, which is a continuation of the Cascade Range of Oregon, and whose southern summits are capped with snow. This range gradually de-creases in height, until it declines into hills of moderate elevation. To the east of the California Mountains are the vast sandy plains, of which we know but little, except that they form a wide trackless waste, destitute of every thing that can fit it for the habitation of man or beast.

The soil is as variable as the face of the country. On the coast range of hills there is little to invite the agriculturist, except in some vales of no great extent. These hills are, however, admirably adapted for raising herds and flocks, and are at present the feeding-grounds of numerous deer, elk, &c., to which the short sweet grass and wild oats that are spread over them, afford a plentiful supply of food. No at-tempts have been made to cultivate the northern part of this section, nor is it susceptible of being the seat of any large agricultural operations.

The valleys of the Sacramento, and that of San Juan, are the most fruitful parts of California, particularly the latter, which is capable of producing wheat, Indian corn, rye, oats, &c., with all the fruits of the temperate and many of the tropical climates. It likewise offers fine pasture-grounds for cattle. This region comprises a level plain, from fifteen to twenty miles in width, extending from the bay of San Fran-cisco, beyond the mission of that name, north and south. This may be termed the garden of California; but although several small streams and lakes serve to water it, yet in dry seasons or droughts, not only the crops but the herbage also suffers extremely, and the cattle are deprived of food.

The Sierra affords little scope for cultivation, being much broken, barren, and sandy. It is in places covered with cedar, pine, and oak; but it offers few inducements to the settler. The great valley of Buena Ventura next succeeds, which, although it offers more prospects of profitable cultivation, is by all accounts far inferior to that of San Juan. It lies nearly parallel to the latter, and is watered by the San Joachim river and its branches.

In this valley the Californian Indians principally dwell. The San Joachim receives its waters from the many streams that issue from the Californian range of mountains. These are well wooded, their base being covered with oaks, to which succeeds the red California cedar (Schubertia abertina), and after it, in a still higher region, pines, until the snows are encountered. On the eastern side of this range, there is found very little timber, and in consequence of the want of moisture, trees do not flourish, even on the west side. The inland plain, constituting a large part of Upper California, is, according to all accounts, an arid waste; the few rivers that exist being periodical, and losing themselves in the sandy soil.

Of the latter portion of the country, however, there is little known, and the accounts given of it vary extensively. It has been crossed by seven persons, who differ altogether in respect to its appearance. One declared that the horses and men had not only a scanty supply of water, but were actually nearly famished for want of food; while others have found both grass and water plentiful. The only thing that can reconcile these contradictory statements is, that these different persons had visited the country at different seasons of the year. It seems not at all improbable that the first of these accounts should be the correct one, for we find great aridity throughout the rest of California, and Oregon also. All agree that the middle and extensive portion of this country is destitute of the requisites for supplying the wants of man.

In climate, California varies as much if not even more than in natural features and soil. On the coast range, it has as high a mean temperature in winter as in summer. The latter is in fact the coldest part of the year, owing to the constant prevalence of the northwest winds, which blow with the regularity of a monsoon, and are exceedingly cold, damp, and uncomfortable, rendering fire often necessary for comfort in midsummer. This is, however, but seldom resorted to, and many persons have informed me that they have suffered more from cold at Monterey, than in places of a much higher latitude. The climate thirty miles from the coast undergoes a great change, and in no part of the world is there to be found a finer or more equable one than in the valley of San Juan. It more resembles that of Andalusia, in Spain, than any other, and none can be more salubrious. The cold winds of the coast have become warmed, and have lost their force and violence, though they retain their freshness and purity. This strip of country is that in which the far-famed missions have been established; and the accounts of these have led many to believe that the whole of Upper California was well adapted for agricultural uses. This is not the case, for the small district already pointed out is the only section of country where these advantages are to be found. This valley extends beyond the pueblo of San Juan, or to the eastward of Monterey: it is of no great extent, being about twenty miles long by twelve wide.

The Sierra, which separates the valley of San Juan from that of Buena Ventura, is about one thousand five hundred feet high, barren and sandy. Pines cover its summit, and the climate is exceedingly dry and arid, though cooled by the fresh wind that passes beyond them. Next comes the central valley of Buena Ventura, which is a continuation of the Sacramento, and through which the San Joachim flows. Being confined within the two ranges of mountains, and not having the same causes operating to modify the temperature as the smaller valley of San Juan, the heats of its summer are oppressive, the thermometer ranging, it is said, higher than within the torrid zone, and the heat continuing without cessation.

Although the California Range is covered with snow in close proximity to this valley, it seems to have but little effect in modifying the climate, which is represented as tropical throughout the year. This valley extends as far south as the San Bernardino Mountain. The residents in California say that they have never known the wind to blow from the northeast within thirty miles of the coast.

This state of things may also prevail in the interior, and will naturally prevent the cool stratum of air from descending into the valley, it being carried to the interior by the prevailing winds from an opposite quarter.

In ordinary seasons these valleys are well watered by streams from the mountains, which vary very much in size: they are for some part of the year mere brooks, while during the rainy season, from November to February, they become in some cases impassable. The Sacramento is the largest river in California. One of its branches, Destruction river, takes its rise near Mount Shaste, and was examined throughout the whole of its course by our land party, until it joined the Sacramento: the latter is thought by some to pass through the mountains and join Pitt's river. Pitt's river is said to take its rise to the northeast of the Shaste Mountain, and from the information that I received, extends as far as Pitt's Lake, under the forty-second parallel. I have reason to doubt whether the length of its course is so great, and believe that the Sacramento has its source in the eastern spurs of the Shaste Mountain. I have, however, indicated by a dotted line on the map, the course Pitt's river is thought to pursue before it joins the Sacramento, This, if correct, would give the Sacramento, with its branches, a course of two hundred miles from the ocean.

The first branch of any size in descending the Sacramento is that called Feather river, which joins it below the Prairie Butes, coming from the northeast. This branch takes its rise in the California Mountains, near their northern end, and has a course of about forty miles. The American river is a small branch that joins the Sacramento at New Helvetia. After receiving this stream, the Sacramento is joined by the San Joachim, which courses from the south, and below their confluence enters the bay of San Pablo through the Straits of Kaquines, thence passing into the bay of San Francisco.

It is navigable for boats to the distance of one hundred and fifty miles, and for vessels as far as New Helvetia. The upper portion of it, near the Prairie Butes, overflows its banks, and submerges the whole of the Sacramento Valley as far down as the San Joachim. This inundation is probably caused by the united effects of the Sacramento and Feather rivers, as there is not in its bed sufficient room to discharge so large a quantity of water. This valley will be presently spoken of in connexion with its survey.

The San Joachim does not pass through the Tula Lake, as laid down by Coultier; its sources are in the Californian Range. The Tula Lake is called by the Indians, Chintache Lake; it is for the most part separated from the channel of the river, but when full joins it.

There are many small streams that flow through the different valleys, and afford partial opportunities for irrigating the land; but there are none of them navigable, except the Sacramento.

Upper California may boast of one of the finest, if not the very best harbour in the world,—that of San Francisco, as before described. Few are more extensive or could be as readily defended as it; while the combined fleets of all the naval powers of Europe might moor in it. This is, however, the only really good harbour which this country possesses; for the others so called may be frequented only during the fine season, being nothing more than roadsteads, affording little safety and but few supplies to vessels.

Among these bays are that of Monterey, the capital of Upper California, and that of Santa Barbara and San Pedro. The last two are partly protected from the swell of the Pacific Ocean by the islands that cover them. They are, however, but seldom used, there being comparatively little trade upon all this coast; for the hides and tallow which formerly abounded and made the business profitable for vessels, are no longer to be procured. The destruction of the missions, and the onerous laws, duties, and prohibitions, have nearly destroyed the little traffic that once existed, and it is now all transferred to the bay of San Francisco. There a few hulks may be seen lying, furnished with every needful article: these keep up an illicit intercourse by the connivance of the officers of the customs, by whose cupidity the revenue laws are openly infringed, and what of right belongs to the government, goes to enrich the governor and his officers.

The principal articles imported, are cotton cloths, velvet, silks, brandies, wines, teas, &c.; in return for which they receive hides and tallow, skins, wheat, and salmon. The attention of the inhabitants has been principally directed to the raising of cattle, and the greater part of the wealth of California may be considered as consisting of live-stock. The exportations, on the average of years, is about one hundred and fifty thousand hides, and two hundred thousand arrobas of tallow. The standard price for the former is two dollars, while the latter is worth one dollar and fifty cents the arroba. A few beaver-skins are obtained, which do not exceed two thousand, and are valued at two dollars apiece. From four to five hundred sea-otter skins are brought in by the American hunters, which are valued at thirty dollars each. Wheat has been exported to the Russian posts, to the amount of twelve thousand bushels, of which the average price is about fifty cents a bushel. Of late, however, it has risen to two dollars and fifty cents, in consequence of the great drought that has prevailed. Among the exports may be also enumerated about three thousand elk and deer skins, which are valued at from fifty cents to a dollar each. The whole merchantable products may be estimated at less than a million of dollars.

The yield of wheat is remarkable, and in some places, where the land is well situated, very large returns are received. Mr. Spears, of Yerba Buena, informed me that he had delivered to an active American farmer thirty bushels of wheat for seed, at a time when it was difficult to procure it, under an agreement that he should have the refusal of the crop at the market price. In the July following, he delivered him three thousand bushels, and on its delivery, he found that the farmer had reserved six hundred bushels for himself; and this without estimating the loss from bad reaping and treading out with horses, would give one hundred and twenty for one. This is not considered a fair criterion or average, as the land was remarkable for its richness and was well attended to; but Mr. Spears and several others assured me that the average would be as high as eighty bushels yielded for one planted.

Indian corn yields well, as also potatoes, beans, and peas. The cultivation of vegetables is increasing rapidly, and supplies in these latter articles may be had in abundance and of the finest quality.

The country appears to be well adapted for grapes. Those that have been tried at the missions yield most abundantly; and about two hundred casks, each of eighteen gallons, of brandy, and the same quantity of wine, are made. The cultivation of the grape increases yearly, but is not sufficient for the supply of the country, as large quantities of foreign wines and liquors are imported, which pay an enormous duty; and although California may not boast of its dense population, every intelligent person I met with agreed that it consumed more spirits in proportion than any other part of the world. Brandy sells for sixty to seventy dollars the cask, or four dollars a gallon, while the price of wine is only eighteen dollars. The wine of the country which I tasted is miserable stuff, and would scarcely be taken for the juice of the grape.

The salmon-fishery, if attended to, would be a source of considerable profit, yet I was told that the Californians never seem disposed to attempt to take them. The general opinion is, that they are too indolent to bestir themselves, and they naturally choose the employment which gives them the least trouble. Above every thing, the rearing of cattle requires the least labour in this country, for it is only necessary to provide keepers and have their cattle marked. This done, they can support themselves by the increase of the stock. At the missions, the manufacture of various coarse articles had been undertaken by the missionaries as a step in the education of the neophytes. Among these were blankets and wearing apparel sufficient to supply all the Indians; but, with the decline of these establishments, the manufactures have in great part been discontinued. Soap of a good quality is manufactured in considerable quantities, and it is thought that it might be exported at a profit, if the proper arrangements were made to use the grease that is now thrown away. The necessary alkali is very abundant. Leather of an excellent quality is also made and well tanned, but in such small quantities as to be hardly sufficient to supply the wants of the country.

There are in California only two or three water-mills for grinding flour, and these are owned by foreigners. The mills in general use in the country, are composed of no more than two burr-stones. To the upper stone a cross-beam is secured, to which mule-power is applied. In most of the estancias there is to be found a mill in an apartment adjoining the kitchen, if not in it. The whole is as primitive as well can be, although I have no doubt it answers all the wants of this rude and indolent people.

From all accounts, besides cattle, the country is well adapted for the raising of sheep, which simply require watching, as they can find plenty of nutritious food the whole year round; but there has been no attention paid to this sort of stock, and the wool is of very ordinary quality. The mutton is thought to be of very fine flavour. The usual price for a sheep is from one dollar and fifty cents to two dollars, when a choice is made for killing.

Hogs are raised in some parts, and might be fed to great advantage on the acorns which are abundant on the hills where the land is not susceptible of cultivation. Pork may be packed at three dollars the hundred-weight. What adds to the facility of doing this business, is the fact that large quantities of salt collect in the ponds in the dry season, which may be obtained for the expense of carting it.

As respects trade, it may be said there is scarcely any, for it is so interrupted, and so much under the influence of the governor and the officers of the customs, that those attempting to carry on any under the forms usual elsewhere, would probably find it a losing business. Foreigners, however, contrive to evade this by keeping their vessels at anchor, and selling a large portion of their cargoes from on board. Great partiality is shown to those of them who have a full understanding with his excellency the governor; and from what I was given to understand, if this be not secured, the traders are liable to exactions and vexations without number. The enormous duties, often amounting to eighty per cent. ad valorem, cause much dissatisfaction on the part of the consumers: the whole amount raised is about two hundred thousand dollars per annum, which is found barely sufficient to pay the salaries of the officers, and defray the costs of the government feasts, which are frequent, and usually cost a thousand dollars each. These emoluments are shared among the heads of departments at Monterey, whilst the soldiers are often for months without their pay, and are made to take it in whatever currency it may suit the government to give. Besides the above duties, there is a municipal tax on many things: thus, a dollar is demanded on every gallon of spirits imported; fifty cents on each beaver or otter skin, and on other articles in the same ratio. Next come the church tithes, which are enormous. I heard of a farmer who was made to pay one hundred and ninety dollars as the tithe on his produce, although he lives far removed from either church or priest. All these things are bringing the government into great disrepute, and the governor is every day becoming more and more unpopular; so much so, that his orders have not been complied with, and have been treated with contempt, particularly when he desires to recruit his forces. A short time before our arrival, he sent a list to a pueblo of the young men to be drafted as soldiers; when it was received, they in a body refused to go, and sent back the disrespectful and defying message, that he might come and take them.

Nothing can be in a worse state than the lower offices, such as the alcaldes, &c. They are now held by ignorant men, who have no ideas of justice, which is generally administered according to the alcalde's individual notions, as his feelings may be enlisted, or the standing of the parties. To recover a debt by legal means, is considered as beyond a possibility, and creditors must wait until the debtor is disposed to pay. Fortunately, and to the honour of the country, a just claim is rarely or never denied; and, until lately, the word of a Californian was sufficient to insure the payment of claims on him; but, such has been the moral degradation to which the people have fallen since the missions have been robbed by the authorities, and the old priests driven out, that no reliance can be placed now upon their promises, and all those who have of late trusted them, complain that engagements are not regarded, and that it is next to impossible to obtain any returns for goods that have been delivered. The state of the country is, however, some excuse, as it has been impossible for any one to make calculations under the existing anarchy and confusion.

It was at first believed that the revolution which took place in November 1836, would result in much immediate good to those who effected it; but such has not been the case. Foreigners unquestionably performed a large part in planning and carrying the change out; yet none have suffered so much by it as they have.

Much of this derangement of business has grown out of the state of the country for the last twenty years; and, although its history is of little importance, a succinct sketch of it may not be wholly devoid of interest. The facts are derived both from Californian and Mexican authorities, as well as from Americans; and, although the accounts frequently differ in some particulars, yet as to the main points they agree.

Previous to the year of the revolution by which California was separated from old Spain (1823), the whole country may be said to have been under the rule of the missions, and the padres who were at their head had acquired a vast influence over the Indians, as well as amongst the soldiery who were placed in the presidios as the guards and protectors of the missions. There were twenty-one missions, and only four presidios. The power of the governors was usually rather nominal than real, and the troops, from being totally neglected, were dependent upon the missions almost for their daily bread. Fortunately for the country, the padres and rulers of the missions were men well adapted for their calling: good managers, sincere Christians, they exerted a salutary influence over all in any way connected with them, practising at the same time the proper virtues of their calling, in order more effectually to inculcate them upon others. These reverend men were all old Spainards, and greatly attached to their king and country. When the revolution broke out, they declined taking the oath to the new government: many, in consequence, left their missions and retired from the country, and some of the others have since died.

Thus, at the same time with a change of rulers, the country was deprived of the religious establishments upon which its society and good order were founded. Anarchy and confusion began to reign, and the want of authority was every where felt. Some of the missions were deserted; the property which had been amassed in them was dissipated, and the Indians turned off to seek their native wilds.

At the time of the separation from Spain, a Californian, by name Arguello, was governor. On his being appointed to that office, one Noniga, a Spanish officer, disliking to be commanded by a Californian, attempted to oppose him. In order to silence this opposition, Noniga was put in command of the presidio of Santa Barbara, where, owing to his misconduct, he was soon dismissed, upon which he again sought to excite the Mexicans against the Californians, and to impress them with the same deadly hatred which he himself felt. With this intent, he omitted no opportunity to represent the actions and conduct of the Californian authorities in the most odious light.

The government of Mexico saw the evils that they had occasioned, when it was too late, and set about remedying them, as well as to fill the vacancies that had occurred. For this purpose, they were disposed to consult the old padres, and offered those who remained, the choice of the northern or southern section, that they might be united in a body. The old Spanish priests chose the southern missions; and the few establishments which lie to the north of San Miguel, were assigned to those from the college of Xacatecas, in Mexico.

By this time the supreme government became convinced that although they had apparently adopted the best mode of palliating the injury the missions had received, yet it had served rather to increase the difficulty. The new Mexican priests were in every way inferior to the old Spainards, neither possessing their intelligence, their skill in governing, their correct principles, nor their dignity of deportment; in short, they were totally unfit for their situation.

In 1825, the supreme government appointed Don Jose Echandia, a Mexican, to succeed Arguello as governor; and he gave universal satisfaction, till 1829, when a revolt took place among the Californians and Indians in the garrison of Monterey, in consequence of their not receiving the arrears of pay that were due them. The governor, with becoming energy, put down this disturbance, and restored order.

In 1831, Echandia was succeeded by Don Manuel Victoria, who changed the whole policy of his predecessor. He became at once, from his tyrannical conduct, extremely unpopular, and in the first year of his administration was so severely wounded in a skirmish at Los Angelos, as to be incapable of continuing in the command. The insurrection, of which this skirmish was an incident, was the most serious that had occurred. It owed its formidable character, as was believed, to the aid which the foreigners gave the Californians: this was the first time the former had interfered with the affairs of the country.

After this event, General Figueroa, who was sent to rule over Upper California, by his mild yet firm deportment, reconciled opinions, and put down all opposition. His administration is still spoken of as having been conducted with great ability and moderation. By his recommendation, the supreme government had sent out a colony of two hundred labourers and agriculturists, of which the country was much in want, to Monterey; but instead of their being what Figueroa had asked for, as such as was reported to have been sent, they turned out to be mere idlers, who had been living at the public expense. The arrival of this colony produced the most unhappy effects, and with them arose an enmity between the Californians and Mexicans, that has acquired additional acrimony from the favour shown the latter by the succeeding governors. Figueroa died in 1835, greatly regretted by all: his death proved a great loss to the country, for, had he lived, things would probably have turned out favourably.

Colonel Chico, the next in command, succeeded Figueroa, but was ill-suited for the situation, and the contrast between him and his predecessor was too perceptible for him to give satisfaction; his conduct towards the inhabitants tended to increase the unfavourable impressions he had first made. It was not long before a dispute arose between him and the supreme judge of the district, upon the question as to which of them the chief authority belonged. Parties became very violent, and Chico determined to put down all opposition by military force. This course gave great dissatisfaction, and coupled with his arbitrary conduct towards the inhabitants and the missions, created a determination to resist him if he did not resign. A letter was written to him to that effect, upon which he felt himself compelled to deliver over the reins of government into the hands of a successor, to avoid the difficulties and dangers to which he would otherwise have been liable,

The next in command was Don Nicolas Gutierez, a lieutenant-colonel: under this officer tranquillity was apparently restored for a time.

During the preceding years, many foreigners had settled in California, who had taken a part in its affairs. These included natives of all countries; and among them were to be found Americans, who had led the lives of hunters and trappers, some of whom had been living in the Rocky Mountains, and on the Columbia river, whilst others had come from Mexico. These persons were naturally of a restless disposition, and disposed to engage in any thing that would produce excitement; bold and reckless in their disposition, they could not remain quiet under the turn things were taking in California, and they now joined and instigated the party opposed to the governor. They argued that California ought to form itself into a free state, by declaring its independence of Mexico, which had not the power to govern it. At that time any plausible arguments had weight with so ignorant a people as the Californians, and this idea was rendered acceptable by the ill-will they bore the Mexicans, and the obvious want of legitimate power. The project of overturning the government was also entertained by those who had previously held office, and particularly by the administrador of the customs, Ramierez, and Cosme Penné, a drunken lawyer, who was the assessor. They were both Mexicans by birth, and belonged to the ultra liberals. With them was joined the inspector, Alvarado, who was extremely popular with the foreigners. The two former, knowing the ignorance that prevailed among the Californians, constituted themselves leaders, and expected, in the event of any change, to be benefited by it; but at the same time they looked with some degree of mistrust and jealously upon the foreigners resident there.

Under such circumstances, the least difficulty was sufficient to bring about a revolution, and it was not long before one occurred that caused an outbreak, and ended in the overthrow of the authorities. About the beginning of November 1836, a dispute arose between the governor and Alvarado, the inspector of the customs, who was threatened with arrest. The popularity of Alvarado with the foreigners caused them at once to take a warm interest in his behalf; and, without inquiring into the right or wrong of the business, they espoused his cause. Alvarado fled to the country, and raised the standard of revolt in the pueblo of San Juan, some leagues from Monterey. The people of California being naturally lazy, ignorant, and indifferent, required some strong stimulus to arouse them; but this was affected, and in consequence of the dissoluteness of the priesthood, and the loss of clerical influence with the lower orders, which ten years of their bad management of the missions had brought about, they were quite unable to restrain the people. It has even been alleged that they favoured the design, in order to have a change, and avoid the heavy exactions that had been made upon them of late by the governor. Be this so or not, there was either no exertion made by the clergy in favour of the government, or their power was too insignificant to be effective.

The people were easily persuaded that a shameful misappropriation of public funds had taken place, and that the robbery of the missions was still going on. The discovery that Chico, who, as has been stated, was forced to resign in favour of the then governor, had defrauded the troops of their pay, and the missions of twenty thousand dollars, satisfied every one that such embezzlement was going on, and furnished a powerful incentive to many to join the standard of Alvarado. He was now acting under the advice and by the directions of the foreigners, who declared their intentions to be—1st. To hoist a new flag, and declare California independent of Mexico. 2d. To banish all Mexicans. 3d. That California should be declared an independent state; and 4th. That all foreigners then under arms, or who took part in the revolution, should be declared citizens. These declarations, although they had the desired effect, were evidently made rather to satisfy the foreigners than to please the natives, and are supposed to have emanated from the administrador Ramierez, and Penné. These men, the most able of the Californians, were desirous to make use of the foreigners to gain their own ends, in which they so far succeeded, that although the foreigners were, in regard to fighting, the prominent actors in the revolution, the result proved that they were but tools employed to gain the ulterior ends of these two designing persons.

Alvarado was now directed to move forward towards Monterey, which from all accounts he was of himself unwilling to do; but the directors of his movements impelled him forward. Who these were, is not well known; but the presumption is, that various citizens of the United States, as well as of England, advised and gave him promises of aid. On the 2d of November, he arrived with his force at Monterey; it consisted of about two hundred men, of whom twenty-five were American hunters, the only part of his force that was effective. Some accounts give a smaller number, and state it at less than half of this. Gutierez, believing the Presidio impregnable, shut himself up in it with about one hundred and seventy persons, sixty of whom were regular soldiers.

The Presidio was at once invested, the beach taken possession of, and a communication opened with several American vessels then lying in the bay. The energy and activity exhibited by Alvarado's party indicated that their movements were directed by others than Spainards or Californians.

Gutierez seems to have proved himself weak and imbecile in allowing these advantages to be obtained without making any endeavours to attack the insurgents. It is said, however, (and his actions certainly give some countenance to the idea,) that the dread in which the American hunters were held by himself and men, prevented his making any effective effort: in fact, their fame for skill in the use of the rifle was known and duly appreciated.

On the 3d, the insurgents were found to be in possession of some cannon, which they established on a neighbouring height, and were amply supplied with ammunition. As it was known that neither arms of this kind nor gunpowder were on shore, there is little doubt that they obtained them from the vessels in the bay; and those who were likley to reap the most advantage from a change in the administration of affairs, were suspected of aiding the insurgents with the means that rendered them, in point of equipment, superior to their adversaries.

On the 4th, Gutierez received an official letter, demanding the surrender of the Presidio and every thing in it. Previous to this, he had determined to resist until the last; but on inquiry, he found that various means had been used to win over the soldiers, who were already disaffected on account of the arrearages of pay due to them. To capitulate was now the only thing to be done; but it was necessary for him to call a council of his officers and deliberate upon the terms offered, or submit to the place being stormed. It is said that this council wore away the whole night, in propositions how they could avoid a surrender or obtain relief, without coming to any conclusion.

At dawn on the 5th, their hunter adversaries becoming impatient at the delay, fired an eighteen-pound ball, which struck the centre of the roof of the Presidio, directly over the apartment where the council was held. This messenger brought them to a quick decision, and in a few minutes a flag of truce was sent out, surrendering unconditionally.

At ten o'clock, the deputation which had been appointed, consisting of Alvarado, Castro, and two ignorant Rancheros, marched in with their force, accompanied, it is said, by some American masters of vessels who were in port. Gutierez and his followers laid down their arms and accepted the stipulations; which were a guarantee of life to himself and officers, and that those who chose might either remain in the country or be suffered to depart. The Mexican flag was now hauled down; when the courage of Alvarado and the deputation failed them, and they refused to hoist the flag of California, which had been prepared for the occasion, and was then ready to be displayed, without first holding a council. This was supposed to be done through the advice of Ramierez and Cosme Penné, who now found that the affair had reached the point they desired, and that it was necessary to prevent any further act in favour of the foreigners. The council was accordingly held, and Miguel Ramierez and Cosme Penné were both allowed to be present. The four articles of declarations formally made, and that have been above recited, were read over for the purpose of being considered and adopted; when these two stated it was not according to their understanding of the plan agreed upon: that it was not to declare the country altogether free and independent of Mexico, but only until the constitution of 1824 should be established. Upon this, the members of the deputation, who were perfectly ignorant of their duties or business, simply answered: "Well, very well; it is just what we wanted: some persons who have longer heads than any of us to put us in the right way and help us better out of the scrape we have got into." Don Cosme immediately took advantage of this, and gave the watchword, "Viva California libre, y muerte a la centralism!"—upon which the Mexican flag was again hoisted. This produced much dissatisfaction among the foreigners, and the fear of them prevented Ramierez and Cosmo Penné from going farther. In the selection of officers, Alvarado was nominated as governor, by Castro; General Vallejo, as commandant-general; Castro, as lieutenant-colonel of the militia; and the inebriate Cosme Penné, as secretary of state.

This proved satisfactory to the foreigners, although it was not what they wished: but the act removing one-half the duties was still more so.

It was soon determined that the Mexicans ought to be removed at once out of the country, notwithstanding the stipulations of the surrender to the contrary. Accordingly, the British brig Clementine was chartered, in which Gutierez and all his officers, with a large number of his men, were embarked, and ordered to be landed at Cape San Lucas, the southern point of Lower California.

Thus in a few days were the authorities changed, without a single gun being fired but the one above spoken of, and without any blood-shed whatever. At the time of despatching the Clementine, Alvarado, with the advice of Cosme and Ramierez, purchased a small schooner, and sent her at once to a port in Mexico to inform the supreme govern-ment of every thing that had taken place, adding that they were willing to remain in allegiance, if they were allowed to choose their own officers. In the mean time they sent commissioners to demand that the other presidios should be given up, and that the inhabitants should acknowledge the authority of those who had overturned the govern-ment. This the officers and inhabitants refused to do, upon which Alvarado marched against Santa Barbara with his rancheros, for the hunters had, for the most part, left him. He was met by a superior force, commanded by a former deputy, named Castillo; but the schooner returned previous to hostilities being commenced, bringing not only a confirmation of the appointment of Alvarado and the others, but with a supply of arms, ammunition, and clothing for the troops, to the amount of ten thousand dollars. When this became known, Castillo and Alvarado became friends, the former acknowledging the authority of the latter, while Alvarado, it is said, took the oath of allegiance to the central government.

Alvarado now returned to Monterey, where, feeling himself more firmly established in his new office, and having been by this caprice of fortune raised above his deserts, he became arrogant to his countrymen, and alienated the foreigners by whom he had been assisted.

It will scarcely be necessary to say, that by this time the missions had lost all their control over the community. The government had seized upon their lands, and appointed an administrador to take charge of the property (which had been decided under an old Spanish law to belong to the government), as well as to rule over the Indians. From the priests were thus removed all further responsibilities and duties, except those strictly clerical. This act brought about the ruin of the missions. The moral and religious usefulness of the priests had been destroyed before, and now the property that was still left became a prey to the rapacity of the governor, the needy officers, and the ad-ministrador, who have well-nigh consumed all. Some of the missions, that had from forty to eighty thousand head of cattle, are new left with less than two thousand, and are literally going to ruin. They are no more what they once were, the pride of the padres, and the seat of the wealth and prosperity of the country. Moreover, this state of things has left the whole community destitute of any moral guide whatever, and without any sort of religious observance, except by a few individuals past the middle age. Alvarado and General Vallejo have the reputation of being foremost in producing this state of things.

After a short time, it was found that the customs did not produce the required revenue; and the new government, fearing to tax the people and missions too openly, resorted to a renewal of the double duties, before more than two vessels had touched on the coast. Every day produced some restrictions upon the foreigners, who had now become estranged from the existing government that they had assisted to establish. Alvarado, finding his acts disapproved of by them, grew suspicious and jealous of their presence; for he well knew, from the manner of his own elevation, what an effective body they were.

This state of things continued until the month of April, 1840, when Alvarado, anticipating an insurrectionary movement, and knowing the confidence that the aid of the foreigners would give the malcontent Californians, determined to rid the territory of them. For the purpose of obtaining some colour for the violence he intended, an Englishman, by the name of Gardner, was found, who deposed that all the foreigners, from San Francisco to San Diego, or from one extreme of California to the other, a distance of six or seven hundred miles, had conspired to murder the governor and take possession of the country: that an American, by the name of Graham, a trapper from the state of Kentucky, was their leader; and that they were to rendezvous, for the purpose, at Nativetes, the residence of Graham. Colonel Castro was accordingly sent thither, with the prefect, two inferior officers, and fifteen armed soldiers. They proceeded to Nativetes, which is about twenty miles from Monterey; but, as they well knew that Graham was a resolute, strong, and brave man, it was necessary to take great precautions. They therefore chose midnight for their attack, at which hour they reached his farm. On their arrival they forced open the door, and at once fired a volley into the bed where he lay asleep, and so close to it that they set fire to his blankets. Graham was wounded in several places, and badly burnt.

On being thus awakened, he attempted to defend himself, but was overpowered by numbers, inhumanly beaten, and then tied hand and foot. A working-man, who attended the cattle with him, by the name of Shard, also an American, was held down by two men while a third deliberately cut the tendons of his legs with a butcher's knife, and left him to die. Graham was then tied upon a horse, and carried to Monterey, where he was loaded with irons, and placed in a filthy cell;—torn from the property he had accumulated, amounting to four or five thousand dollars in specia, and about ten thousand dollars in cattle, which he had reared and bought, through his own industry: this, it is supposed, fell into the hands of the governor, who was much in want of funds at the time, and could conceive of no way by which his coffers could be so readily replenished as by such a wholesale robbery.

After the arrest of Graham, more than sixty foreigners were taken up immediately, put into irons, and cast into prison with him. At the same time, orders were issued to apprehend every foreigner found upon the coast, and in case of their not giving bonds for their appearance, they were to be thrust into prison.

Forty-seven of these men were embarked in a vessel called the Guipuzcoa, loaded with irons, nearly half of whom are said to have been citizens of the United States. One of these died from the treatment he received; and the hardships they were obliged to undergo on their journey to Tepic, are almost past belief.

The Guipuzcoa was eleven days on her passage to San Blas, during which time the prisoners were kept in the hold of this small vessel, without light or air, and endured every description of ill treatment. On their arrival at San Blas, they were landed without delay, and immediately marched, in the short space of two days, to Tepic, a distance of sixty miles.

The thermometer was at 90°; the road was mountainous and rough; they were barefooted, heavily ironed, and without any food, except what was given them from charity. They were urged forward by lashes inflicted on their naked bodies, and one who sank under the fatigue was severely beaten with the butt-end of a musket.

At Tepic, they found in the English and American consuls kind friends, who exerted themselves to relieve their wants, and finally, through their remonstrances, and those of the English and American ministers, they were allowed to return to California; and orders were given that they should produce certificates of their losses, and be paid for them. All the Englishmen have returned, with every necessary document to establish their claims, and obtain redress for their wrongs; but on the part of the Americans, this is far from being the case. Of them none but Graham have returned, and he is broken both in health and spirits. What remuneration he has received, I did not learn; but the French and English have all obtained indemnity, through the attention their governments have paid to their wrongs. Ours alone has failed in the prompt protection of its citizens; and many complaints are made by our countrymen abroad that the government at home seems to have very little regard for their lives or property.

It would appear by this want of attention on the part of our government, that it had not been fully satisfied that the conduct of its citizens had been correct; at least, that is the feeling among them abroad. I have little testimony on this subject, except the protestations of many of those who have been more or less suspected of taking part in the expected revolt. I can say, that all the accounts I received invariably spoke of the foreigners as having had nothing to do with the intended outbreak, even if it were organized; and every one should be satisfied that they were innocent, by the fact that in Mexico they were all adjudged to be entirely guiltless of the charges brought against them, and that they were sent back at the expense of the Mexican government, with letters of security, and an order making it obligatory on the Governor of California to assist them in procuring evidence of the damages they had sustained. Although this may have been ample satisfaction, so far as mere remuneration goes, yet for the barbarous conduct shown to them by the authorities, some punishment ought to have been inflicted, and an example made. But such has not been the case, and those officers are still kept in their high places, with the power to repeat like barbarities. There is no other way to account for this not being insisted upon, than by supposing that the Mexicans hold so little authority over this territory as to make them extremely scrupulous how they take any measures that may cause the dismemberment of the state, and the loss of even the nominal dominion they now possess.

The situation of Upper California will cause its separation from Mexico before many years. The country between it and Mexico can never be any thing but a barren waste, which precludes all intercourse except that by sea, always more or less interrupted by the course of the winds, and the unhealthfulness of the lower or seaport towns of Mexico. It is very probable that this country will become united with Oregon, with which it will perhaps form a state that is destined to control the destinies of the Pacific. This future state is admirably situated to become a powerful maritime nation, with two of the finest ports in the world,—that within the straits of Juan de Fuca, and San Francisco. These two regions have, in fact, within themselves every thing to make them increase, and keep up an intercourse with the whole of Polynesia, as well as the countries of South America on the one side, and China, the Philippines, New Holland, and New Zealand, on the other. Among the latter, before many years, may be included Japan. Such various climates will furnish the materials for a beneficial interchange of products, and an intercourse that must, in time, become immense; while this western coast, enjoying a climate in many respects superior to any other in the Pacific, possessed as it must be by the Anglo-Norman race, and having none to enter into rivalry with it but the indolent inhabitants of warm climates, is evidently destined to fill a large space in the world's future history.

Although I have already spoken of the Indians, yet in order to make the state of the country fully understood, it is necessary to explain their former connexion with the missions, as well as their present condition.

The Indians who were brought into the fold of the missions, were either induced through persuasion, by force, or enticed by presents: the agreement, or rather law, was, that they should be converted to Christianity; and for this benefit conferred upon them, they were to give ten years' faithful service, after which time they were to be at liberty, and to have allotted to them a small piece of land for cultivation, and a few cattle, provided they could get the security of any respectable person for their good behaviour. This seldom happened; but their treatment was much more kind after the expiration of their term of service, and they usually remained in the employ of the missions, having become attached to their masters and occupations. These chiefly consisted in taking care of cattle, the work of the farm, gardening, and household duties. Some became carpenters and blacksmiths; others weavers, shoemakers, and manufacturers of leather; and some were let out to private service to "gente de razon," or people of reason, as the whites are termed. The police of the missions were strict, and punishment was administered when required; but then rewards for good behaviour were also given, as well as for bringing in neophytes. In the latter way, it is said that the missions were usually recruited.

During the troubles of 1836, the Indians of many of the missions were cast off neglected, and in fact deprived of the proceeds of their labour. They had reason to believe, as had been impressed upon them by the Spanish padres, that they were interested in the proceeds and wealth that had been accumulated by their labour; and this belief had naturally tended to attach them to the soil.

The ravages of the small-pox, two years prior to our visit, completed the destruction of these establishments; for it swept off one-half of the Indians, and served to dispirit the rest. Many of them have joined the wild Indians, and are now committing acts of violence on the whites; they are becoming daily more daring, and have rendered a residence in single farm-houses or estancias not without danger. In looking at the state in which these poor Indians have been left, it cannot be denied but that they have cause to be dissatisfied with the treatment they have received.

Every mission was regarded as a separate family of Indians, and some of these included twelve hundred individuals. During the management of the Spanish priests, every thing was judiciously conducted: the Indians were well dressed, well fed, and happy; out of their earnings the priests were able to buy annually ten thousand dollars' worth of articles for their wants and gratification, from the vessels trading upon the coast. Each mission formed a body politic of itself, having its own alcalde, inferior officers, &c., and every thing went on prosperously. The Indians, though at first disinclined to work, soon became industrious, when they found the benefits and advantages that accrued to themselves, and became converts to Christianity, so far as forms went, in order to entitle them to its presents. It is not surprising that a rapid increase of wealth took place, considering the number of labourers in the field, added to a rich soil and fine climate.

As has been before stated, in 1835, orders from the supreme government were issued, administrators were appointed to each mission, and the priests were deprived of their sway, leaving them only their clerical duties to attend to, with a small stipend. So far as they were personally concerned, this was deserved; for, with but one or two exceptions, their lives were entirely opposite to what they ought to have been; they were openly and publicly dissolute. The administrators have made themselves and those by whom they were appointed, rich upon the spoils of these missions; and so great have been the drafts upon some of these missions, that they have not been able to support their neophytes. The mission of San Jose, for instance, during the year of our visit, was obliged to order off five hundred of its proselytes, to procure their subsistence as they best could. These acts seem to be committed without any kind of consideration, or idea that there is any injustice practised: the property acquired by the missions is looked upon as belonging to the state; the claims of the Indians are entirely overlooked, and in the event of their taking the cattle that in truth belong to them, they are severely punished. This naturally irritates them, for not only can they perceive the injustice of others appropriating the fruits of their labour, but are exasperated by seeing them living upon the common stock, while they are obliged to seek a precarious subsistence in the forest.

In consequence of this state of things, depredations are continually committed by the Indians; and, a month previous to the arrival of the squadron, they had driven off three hundred horses. Retaliatory measures on the part of the Californians were adopted; a party was collected and despatched to punish them, which proceeded towards the interior, came to a village, and without any inquiry whether its dwellers had been the aggressors, it was set on fire, and reduced to ashes; some of the defenseless old men, who from their infirmities could not escape, were put to death, and forty or fifty women and children carried off as prisoners. This was not all: these prisoners were apportioned as slaves to various families, with whom they still remain in servitude, and receive very harsh treatment. Smarting under such wrongs, it is not surprising that the Indians should retaliate. They openly assert that after taking all the horses, they will commence with families; and many of those which are situated on the frontiers, experience much alarm. In June 1841, an Englishman was shot by an arrow at the door of his house, early in the evening. The Indians enticed him out by making a noise near by, and the moment he opened the door, with a candle in his hand, an arrow was sent through his heart.

The Indians at present rarely steal any thing but horses; but so daring are they, that they not unfrequently take them out of the enclosures near the pueblos. Their reason for confining themselves to this description of property is, that with them they are able to avoid pursuit, which would not be the case if they took cattle. The Californians, on detecting and apprehending the aggressors, show them no mercy, and their lives are made the forfeit. This constant foray on one side or the other keeps up a continual embitterment, and as long as the present imbecile government lasts, this state of things must every day grow worse, and will undoubtedly tend to affect the value of property, as well as to prevent immigration, and settlement in the country.

To all strangers but those of the Spanish race, the Indians seem in general well disposed, as they have usually received from the former considerate and kind treatment. The character of these Indians is not represented as savage, and they were little disposed to trouble the whites until they had been themselves ejected from the missions, and forced to consort with those who are yet in a wild state. The knowledge they have of the Californians, of the missionary establishments, and the manner of conducting them, enables them to act more effectively; and if it were not for the presence of the English and Americans, they would either drive the Spanish race out of the country, or confine them to the narrow limits of their villages.

The number of Indians is variously stated, at from twelve to fifteen thousand; but it is believed by some of the best informed, that their number, since the small-pox made its ravages among them, is not much more than one-half of this number, or eight or nine thousand. The principal part of these are the tribes on the Sacramento.

In like manner, there has been an exaggeration in the computation of the number of the whites, or gente de razon. These have been usually estimated at five thousand; but, from the best information, I could not satisfy myself that they number more than three thousand souls. In this estimate is not included those of mixed blood, who may amount to two thousand more; so that in the whole of Upper California, at the date of our visit, the entire population was about fifteen thousand souls; and this estimate cannot be far from the truth.

The health and robustness of the white inhabitants seem remarkable, and must be attributed to the fine climate, as well as to their simple diet. This consists of beef roasted upon the coals, a few vegetables, and the tortilla, which is a thin cake, made of corn-meal, and baked upon a sheet of iron. Throughout the country, both with the rich and poor, this is the general fare; but some few luxuries have been lately introduced, among which are rice and tea. The latter is used so sparingly, that the discoloration of the water is scarcely perceptible. At the missions they live more after the Spanish fashion. The children are, for the most part, left to take care of themselves, and run about naked and dirty. They are generally robust, and their relative number seems to be very great; thus, it is by no means uncommon to see families of fourteen or fifteen children; and an instance was mentioned to me of a woman near Yerba Buena, who had had twenty-six. A large number die from accidental falls from horses, with which from their earliest childhood they are accustomed to be engaged. They early become expert and fearless riders, and this skill is not confined altogether to the male sex; the women are almost equally expert. Families with numerous members are seldom met with who have not had to mourn the loss of several of their number from casualties of this sort.

Although the Californians are comparatively few in number, yet they have a distinctive character. Descended from the old Spaniards, they are unfortunately found to have all their vices, without a proper share of their virtues; they are exceedingly fond of gambling, which is equally in favour with the male and female portion of the community. Their games consist in cards, dice, &c.

Their amusements are cock-fighting, bull and bear-baiting, and dancing; these are the predominant occupations of their lives, always accompanied with excessive drinking. Parties of amusement, to which the surrounding population is invited, are frequent; these generally last for three days, and rarely break up without some quarrel. Weddings are particularly liable to these disorders, and at each of the three last that took place at and in the vicinity of Yerba Buena, previous to our visit there, a life was lost by the cuchillo. This weapon is always worn, and is promptly resorted to in all their quarrels.

The female portion of the community are ignorant, degraded, and the slaves of their husbands. They are very fond of dress, and will make any sacrifice, even their own honour, to gratify it. The men have no trades, and depend for every thing upon the Indians at the missions, some of whom are quite ingenious, both as carpenters and blacksmiths. The whites are so indolent, and withal have so much pride, as to make them look upon all manual labour as degrading; in truth, they regard all those who work as beneath them; they, in consequence, can never be induced to labour. An anecdote was related to me of one who had been known to dispense with his dinner, although the food was but a few yards off, because the Indian was not at hand to bring it to him.

The state of morals here is very low, and is every day becoming worse. During the residence of the old Spanish priests, the people were kept under some control; but since the change I have narrated, priest and layman are alike given up to idleness and debauchery. One thing they are said to be remarkable for, which is their extreme hospitality: it is alleged that they will give up all business to entertain a guest. They put no value whatever upon time, and in entering into contracts they have no regard to punctuality, frequently allowing two, three, and four years to pass before payment. This does not proceed from dishonesty, or any intention to evade their debts, for eventually they pay, if they can, and do not object to the amount of interest. They in fact regard the inconvenience to which they may have put their creditors as of no sort of consequence.

I understood that to offer money for entertainment was considered as an insult; but I did it notwithstanding, and although it was refused from myself, yet, when made through my servant, it was readily accepted. While one is entertained by them, if he should want to hire or purchase any thing, the landlord will league with those about him in schemes of extortion to be practised upon the stranger, and appear vexed with those who are the prominent extortioners. Instances of this will be given hereafter.

The Californians, as a people, must be termed cruel in their treatment to their wives, as well as to the Indians; and in a still greater degree, of course, to their slaves and cattle. They are exceedingly ignorant of every thing but extortion, riding horses, and catching bullocks.

Having thus thrown together the general information I was able to procure, I shall proceed to speak more particularly of our operations in the country, and intercourse with the inhabitants.

On the 20th of August, Lieutenant-Commandant Ringgold left the Vincennes with six boats, accompanied by Dr. Pickering, Lieutenants Alden and Budd, Passed Midshipman Sandford, Midshipmen Hammersly and Elliott, and Gunner Williamson, with provisions for thirty days, accompanied by an Indian pilot. They first passed the islands of Angelos and Molate, next the points of San Pedro and San Pablo, and then entered the bay of San Pablo.

This bay is of a form nearly circular, and ten miles in diameter; many small streams enter it on all sides, from the neighbouring hills. On the east side of this bay, the river Sacramento empties into it through the Straits of Kaquines. The land is high, and the sandstone rock on each side of the straits resembles that seen about the Straits of De Fuca. The hills are thickly covered with wild oats, which were ripe, and the landscape had that peculiar golden hue before remarked. The contrast of this with the dark green foliage of the scattered oaks, heightens the effect, which, although peculiar, is not unpleasing to the sight. The trees all have an inclination towards the southeast, showing the prevalence and violence of the bleak northwest winds, producing on them a gnarled and mountain character. This feature is general throughout the coast of California, and gives the trees a singular appearance, the flat tops having the air of being cut or trimmed after the manner of box trees. The tops are bent to one side, and the larger branches hidden by the numerous twigs which compose the mass. The only place where a similar character was observed by us impressed upon the foliage, was at Terra del Fuego.

After passing the straits, the delta of the Sacramento opened to view. The Tula marshes, which are overflowed by the river above, are very extensive, and are said to be the resort of a vast number of beavers, which, in consequence of the nature of the ground, are difficult to catch, many more traps being necessary than in other localities.

The party took the southeast arm of the Sacramento, and proceeded up the stream for the distance of three miles, where they encamped, without water, that of the river being still brackish. The soil was hard, from being sunburnt, and the foot-marks of the cattle, which had been made during the last rainy season, still remained.

In the morning, they discovered that they had taken the wrong branch of the river, for this led immediately into the San Joachim. They, in consequence, returned to the entrance, where they began their survey. On the 23d, they reached the residence of Captain Suter, and encamped on the opposite bank.

Captain Suter is a Swiss by birth, and informed them that he had been a lieutenant in the Swiss guards during the time of Charles X. Soon after the revolution of July, he came to the United States, and passed several years in the state of Missouri. He has but recently removed to California, where he has obtained from the government a conditional grant of thirty leagues square, bounded by the Sacramento on the west, and extending as far up the river as the Prairie Butes. The spot he has chosen for the erection of his dwelling and fortification, he has called New Helvetia; it is situated on the summit of a small knoll, rising from the level prairie, two miles from the east bank of the Sacramento, and fifty miles from its mouth. New Helvetia is bounded on the north by the American Fork, a small serpentine stream, which has a course of but a few miles. This river, having a bar near its mouth, no vessels larger than boats can enter it. At this place the Sacramento is eight hundred feet wide, and this may be termed the head of its navigation during the dry season, or the stage of low water.

Mr. Geiger, a young American from Newport, is now attached to Captain Suter's establishment; but he informed me that he intended to settle higher up the Sacramento, on the banks of the Feather river. When Captain Suter first settled here in 1839, he was surrounded by some of the most hostile tribes of Indians on the river; but by his energy and management, with the aid of a small party of trappers, has thus far prevented opposition to his plans. He has even succeeded in winning the good-will of the Indians, who are now labouring for him in building houses, and a line of wall, to protect him against the inroads or attacks that he apprehends, more from the present authorities of the land, than from the tribes about him, who are now working in his employ. He holds, by appointment of the government, the office of administrador, and has, according to his own belief, supreme power in his own district, condemning, acquitting, and punishing, as well as marrying and burying those who are under him. He treats the Indians very kindly, and pays them well for their services in trapping and working for him. His object is to attach them, as much as possible, to his interests, that in case of need he may rely upon their chiefs for assistance.

Although Captain Suter is, in general, in the habit of treating the Indians with kindness, yet he related to our gentlemen instances in which he had been obliged to fusilade nine of them; indeed, he does not seem to stand upon much ceremony with those who oppose him in any way. His buildings consist of extensive currals and dwelling-houses, for himself and people, all built of adobes. Labour is paid for in goods. The extent of his stock amounts to about one thousand horses, two thousand five hundred cattle, and about one thousand sheep, many of which are now to be seen around his premises, giving them an appearance of civilization.

Captain Suter has commenced extensive operations in farming; but in the year of our visit the drought had affected him, as well as others, and ruined all his crops. About forty Indians were at work for him, whom he had taught to make adobes. The agreement for their services is usually made with their chiefs, and in this way, as many as are wanted are readily obtained. These chiefs have far more authority over their tribes than those we had seen to the north; and in the opinion of an intelligent American, they have more power over and are more respected by their tribes than those of any other North American Indians. Connected with the establishment, Captain Suter has erected a distillery, in which he makes a kind of pisco from the wild grape of the country.

The duties I have already named might be thought enough for the supervision of one person; but to these must be added the direction of a large party of trappers and hunters, mostly American, who enter here into competition with those of the Hudson Bay Company; and attention to the property of the Russian establishment at Ross and Bodega, which had just been transferred to him for the consideration of thirty thousand dollars. In the purchase were included all the stock, houses, arms, utensils, and cattle, belonging to the establishment. It was understood that this post was abandoned, by orders of the Russian government, the Russian Company no longer having any necessity to hold it to procure supplies, as they are now to be furnished under a contract with the Hudson Bay Company; and by giving it up, they avoid many heavy expenses.

Bodega was first established by the Russians in 1812, under a permission of the then governor of Monterey, to erect a few small huts for salting their beef. A small number of men were left to superintend this business, which in a few years increased, until the place became of such importance in the eyes of the Spanish authorities, that on the Russians attempting to establish themselves at San Francisco,* they were ordered to leave the country. This they refused to do, and having become too strong to be removed by the Spanish force, they had been suffered to remain undisturbed until the time of our visit.

The port of Bodega is situated about ninety miles to the north of that of San Francisco, and being both inconvenient and small, cannot be

* On the island of Yerba Buena, and to employ their men in trapping during the season.

entered except by vessels of a small draft of water. From what I understood from the officers who had been in charge of it, it had been a very considerable expense to the Russian American Company to fortify it; and the disposal of the whole, on almost any terms, must have been advantageous. Captain Suter had commenced removing the stock and transporting the guns, &c., to his establishment.

The buildings at the two posts numbered from fifty to sixty, and they frequently contained a population of four or five hundred souls. Since the breaking up of the establishment, the majority of the Russians returned to Sitka; the rest have remained in the employ of the present owner.

During our stay, there was much apprehension on the part of some that the present governor of the district next west of New Helvetia, felt jealous of the power and influence that Captain Suter was obtaining in the country; and it was thought that had it not been for the force which the latter could bring to oppose any attempt to dislodge him, it would have been tried. In the mean time Captain Suter is using all his energies to render himself impregnable.

In his manners, Captain Suter is frank and prepossessing; he has much intelligence, is conversant with several languages, and withal not a little enthusiastic: he generally wears a kind of undress uniform, with his side-arms buckled around him. He has a wife and daughter whom he expects soon to join him.

New Helvetia was found to be in latitude 38° 33′ 45″ N., and longitude 121° 40′ 05″ W.

According to this gentleman, there are nine different tribes of Indians that are now in his neighbourhood, and within a short distance of his territory.

In the evening our party were favoured with a dance by Indian boys, who, before they began, ornamented themselves with white masks, and decked their bodies each according to his own taste. The music was vocal, and several joined in the song. Their motions were thought to resemble the Pawnees' mode of dancing. Their music was more in harmony than among the other tribes we had seen; neither has their language any of the harsh guttural sounds found in those of the Oregon Indians. Every word of their language appears to terminate with a vowel, after the manner of the Polynesian dialects, which gives their voices much more softness than the tribes to the north, to whom they have no resemblance whatever, though they are said to be somewhat like the Shoshones.

The wear fillets of leaves around their heads, and often tie on them a piece of cotton, after the manner of the Polynesians. These Indians do not build canoes, although they admire and prize them highly; they are excellent swimmers, and in consequence of it do not need them in their narrow streams; they, however, make use of simple rafts, composed of one or two logs, generally split.

The venereal disease is said to prevail to a great extent among them; and whole tribes have been swept off by the small-pox. The former is said to have been communicated by the Indians who have been discharged from the mission. All agree that the Indians have been very unjustly treated by the governor. Cattle that had been given to them by the padres of the mission when they left it, have been taken away from them by this functionary, and added to his own stock—whence a saying has been derived, that the governor's cows produce three times a year. The Spanish laws do not recognise the Indian title to lands, but consider them and the Indians also in the light of public property.

Although the country around was parched up with the severe drought that had prevailed, yet the short grasses were abundant, and it was more completely covered with vegetation than that below. Scattered oaks are seen in all directions, some of which are of large dimensions,—five or six feet in diameter, and sixty or seventy feet high.

The scenery was very much admired, and Mount Diavolo, near the mouth of the San Joachim, adds to its beauty. The mountains to the east are visible from Captain Suter's settlement, and it is said that during some portions of the year they are covered with snow. A route across them was followed, directly east of this place, by a party, but they were twenty days in getting over, and found the country so thickly wooded that they were obliged to cut their way. The pass which is recommended as better, is two hundred miles to the north of this place, through the gap made by the head waters of the Sacramento. This has led to the belief that Pitt's river extends in this direction through and beyond them.

The best route to the United States is to follow the San Joachim for sixty miles, thence easterly, through a gap in the Snowy Mountains, by a good beaten road; thence the course is northeasterly to Mary's river, which flows southeast and has no outlet, but loses itself in a lake; thence continuing in the same direction, the Portneuf river, in the Upper Shoshone, is reached; and thence to Fort Hall. According to Dr. Marsh, (an American of much intelligence, resident at the mouth of the San Joachim, to whom we are indebted for much information of the country,) there is plenty of fresh water and pasturage all the way, and no proper desert between the Californian Range and the Colorado.

Dr. Marsh crossed nothing like a range of mountains in the whole route from the United States. Hills and mountains were often seen on what he calls the table-land of New Mexico. The most common plant met with was an acacia, a small shrub which is also to be found in the southern parts of New Mexico, where the climate is likewise very arid. In one district where it occurs, it is found necessary to protect both horse and rider with a sort of armour against this rigid and thorny vegetation, between latitude 37° and 38° N.

He also reports that there are other streams to the east of the mountains without outlets, and which do not reach the Colorado, although running in that direction. He identifies the Youta, or great Salt Lake, with the Lake Timponogos of the early Spanish fathers who visited it, and agrees with others in placing the north end of it nearly in the parallel of 42° N.

The Colorado he reports to be impracticable for boats to descend from the head waters to its mouth, on account of its rapidity. There is one place in it that is described as similar to the Dalles of the Columbia, which is supposed to be where it passes through the range of mountains.

The banks of the river are bordered with marshes, which extend for miles back. This kind of country continues up both the Sacramento and San Joaquim, and is the proper Tula district of which so much has been said, and so many errors propagated. Here the tula (Scirpus lacustris) grows in great luxuriance.

On the 25th, the boats left New Helvetia. It was discovered, previous to starting, that four men had deserted from their party. This is a common circumstance in this port, and very few vessels visit it without losing some portion of their crews. The dissolute habits of the people form such strong temptations for sailors, that few can resist them. A number of men who were deserters were continually around us. Among others, the sergeant and marine guard that had deserted from H. B. M. ship Sulphur were the most troublesome. Their appearance did not prove that they had changed their situation for the better.

Ten miles up the river, a sand-bar occurred, over which it was found that the launch could not pass. Lieutenant-Commandant Ringgold therefore left her at this place, under charge of Mr. Williams, taking sufficient provisions in the boats. The oaks became more scattered, and the soil thickly covered with vegetation, although parched up by continued drought.

On the 26th, they reached the mouth of Feather river, which is fifteen miles above New Helvetia. It appeared nearly as broad as the main stream, but there is a bar extending the whole distance across it, on which the boats grounded. On the point of the fork, the ground was strewed with the skulls and bones of an Indian tribe, all of whom are said to have died, within a few years, of the tertian fever, and to have nearly become extinct in consequence. Near this had been an Indian village, which was destroyed by Captain Suter and his trappers, because its inhabitants had stolen cattle, &c. The affair resulted in one of the Indians being killed, twenty-seven made captive, and the removal of the remainder beyond the limits of his territory. The battle-ground was pointed out, at a bend of the river, which is only one-third of a mile across, though three around. Above the junction of the two rivers, the Sacramento becomes sensibly diminished.

Game is represented to have decreased in this vicinity, from the numbers destroyed by the parties of the Hudson Bay Company, who annually frequent these grounds. Large flocks of curlew were seen around; and the California quail, which disappeared since leaving the coast, was again seen. The trees that lined the banks consist of the cotton-wood, &c. Single oaks, with short grass beneath them, are scattered over the plain.

The next day, as they advanced, game became more plentiful, and elk were found to be most so. Some of them were of large size, and at this season of the year, the rutting, they are seen generally in pairs; but at other times, the females are in large herds. They are fine-looking animals, with very large antlers, and seemed, in the first instance, devoid of fear. The herds are usually thirty to forty in number, and are chiefly composed of females and their young. The father of the flock is always conspicuous, and with his horns seemed to over-shadow and protect the family.

The tula or bulrush was still found in great quantities, growing on the banks. The Indians use its roots as food, either raw, or mixed with the grass seed, which forms the principal article of their food. This root is likewise eaten by the grisly bear.

At the encamping-place was a grove of poplars of large size, some of which were seventy feet high, and two and a half feet in diameter. The leaf resembled that of the American aspen. At night they had a slight thunder-shower. The wolves and bears had entered the camp during the night, although there was a watch kept at each end of it. The howling of the wolves was almost constant.

On the 27th, the current in the Sacramento had become much more rapid, and the snags more frequent; its banks were on an average about twenty feet above the water, though there was every appearance on them of their having been overflowed. The prairies are perfectly level, and every where overspread with dead shells of the Planorbis. In some places these shells appeared as though they had been collected in heaps. From the top of these banks, the Prairie Butes were in sight to the northward and westward.

As they proceeded up the river, the country continued of the same character, the level being only interrupted by the line of trees that borders the river. These consist of oaks and sycamores.

They encamped at a late hour, on a spot where the prairie had been burnt over, and were much disturbed during the night, by the bears, wolves, and owls. Near this camp was a deserted village.

On the 29th, they for the first time met Indians, who appeared quite shy, concealing themselves behind trees. As they increased in numbers, however, they became more confident, and invited the party to land. Towards noon the character of the country began to change, and trees of a larger size than before were seen, growing out from the banks. A little after noon, they met with the remains of a fish-weir. Some Indians were seen along the banks, armed with bows, arrows, and lances: none but males appeared; they, however, made no hostile demonstrations.

Game and fur-bearing animals had become more numerous, and among them were the lynx and fox. The latter is the species whose fur brings a high price in China, where as much as twenty dollars is paid for a skin. This fox is said to have one peculiarity, namely, that when chased it will ascend trees. Bears were also in great numbers. It is reported that they will sometimes attack and eat the Indians.

Dr. Marsh thinks there is but one species, the grisly bear; but the black bear of the United States is found in New Mexico, and highly prized for its skin; though Dr. Pickering thinks he saw another species, whose summer coat approaches the yellow bear of Oregon. The skin of the young is here sometimes made into quivers, and they are destitute of the horny claws of the grisly bear. The skin of the latter animal is said sometimes to be as large as that of an ox; its food is the same as that of the Indians, and varies with the seasons. Its strength is said to be prodigiously great, and it has been known when lassoed to drag three horses; and when baited in the bull and bear fights practised in California, will check the charge of a bull by putting out one of its paws.

They will also ascend the oaks for the acorns, and break off branches so large as almost to ruin the tree. It has been generally supposed that they do not climb; but all the hunters bear testimony that they can do it, although slowly and clumsily. They are now less numerous than formerly; indeed, it is alleged that the lower country, near the San Joachim, was once so infested with these bears, that the Indians were obliged to keep to the high lands when traveling.

It does not at all times kill its enemies when it has them in its power; rarely attacks a man unless he comes upon him by surprise, and is not considered a dangerous animal.

Anecdotes are told of hunters who had fallen into the power of grisly bears, which would cover them up with brush, grass, and leaves, and put them down, without further molestation, so long as they remained quiet; if they attempted to rise again, the bear would again put them down, cover them over as before, and finally leave them unhurt.

Three or four are usually seen feeding together. The cubs are remarkably small in proportion to the full-grown animal.

Lieutenant-Commandant Ringgold, Dr. Pickering, and Mr. Geiger, landed to procure an interview with the chief, who, with some others, was prevailed upon to accompany them to their encampment. The chief presented them with a tuft of white feathers, stuck on a stick about one foot long, which was supposed to be a token of friendship. These Indians were naked, and some of them had feathers in their hair, arranged in different ways. One among them was seen pitted with the small-pox, which was the only instance that had been observed of the sort. Their fillets of feathers somewhat resembled those worn by the chiefs at the Sandwich Islands; and feather cloaks were seen at the village, resembling some we had seen to the north, near the Straits of De Fuca.

Their bows and arrows were precisely like those described as used by the more northern tribes. The arrows were about three feet long, and the bows were of yew, encased with sinew. Their arrows, as well as their spears, which were very short, were pointed with flint.

These Indians were generally fine robust men, of low stature, and badly formed; but the chiefs, five or six in number, were fully equal in size to the whites, though inferior in stature and good-looking as compared with the generality of the Polynesians. They had a strong resemblance to the latter, except that the nose was not so flat and their colour rather darker. Although the men go naked, the women are said to wear the maro. The males seemed to be exceedingly jealous, on account, it is said, of the unprincipled conduct of the whites who have occasionally passed among them. Their hair is not worn as long as it is by the northern Indians, and is much thicker. They had beards and whiskers an inch or two long, very soft and fine.

One of them was observed to have stuck in his head a long pin or small stick, like that so much in use among the Feejees. Most of them had some slight marks of tattooing on their breast, somewhat similar to that of the Chinooks. Several of them had their ears bored, and wore in the opening round pieces of wood or bone, some of which were carved.

Their rancheria, or village, consisted of no more than five or six huts, built around a larger one, which appeared somewhat like the "tamascals"—sweating-houses. All their houses were formed in the following manner: a round pit is dug, three or four feet deep and from ten to twenty feet in diameter; over this a framework of sticks is raised, woven together, upon which is laid dried grass and reeds; the whole is then covered with earth. They have one small opening, into which it is necessary to creep on all-fours; another is left on the top, which is extended upwards with bundles of grass, to serve as a chimney; in some of the houses there was a kind of hanging-shelf, apparently for the purpose of drying fish. The tamascal differed in no respect from the others, except in its size, and appeared sufficiently large to contain half the inhabitants of the rancheria; but, unlike the rest, it had several instead of one opening; all of these had coverings, which are intended for the purpose of retaining the heat as long as possible. The Indians are particularly fond of these baths, and make constant use of them. The roofs of their houses are strong enough to bear the weight of several persons, and the Indians are usually seen sitting on the top of them. Previous to our gentlemen reaching the rancheria, their women had all decamped, excepting one old one, who, on perceiving the party close to her, dropped her load, and in excessive fear darted off like a wild animal. Around the huts were scattered vast quantities of the mussels' shells and acorns, which would therefore seem to be the principal articles of food. Near the huts, large branches of trees had been stuck up for shade. Some water-tight baskets and bulrush mats were their only fabrics. They do not appear to pay any attention to cultivation, and the only appearance of it was in a species of Cucurbita (mock orange), planted near their village; but what use they made of this was not learned.

This rancheria is said to contain between two and three hundred warriors, who are a fair specimen of the tribes of the country, and are the most troublesome to the trappers, with whom they generally have a fight once a year. On one occasion, the Hudson Bay Company left their cattle in their charge, and when the delivery was demanded they refused to give them up; war was accordingly made on them, and after they had lost forty of their warriors, they consented to return the cattle and make peace. These Indians do not use the tomahawk, nor practise scalping. They go unclothed, even in winter, although the climate is occassionally quite cold in this northern part of the valley.

On the morning when the party were breaking up camp to embark, an Indian boldly seized the bowie-knife-pistol of Dr. Pickering, and made at once for the woods. He had chosen his time well, for no arms were at hand. Several of the men pursued him, but by his alertness he eluded all pursuit; and having gained the bushes, escaped with his prize.

This act, committed in open daylight, and at the risk of life, shows how strong is their propensity to steal. All the other Indians present soon understood the difficulty, and at once took their departure. The chief was not present; those who were concerned in the theft had not been before seen, and it was conjectured, belong to one of the rancherias higher up the river. A short distance above the place where this occurred, they met the chief, to whom the theft was made known, and who promised to restore the stolen article.

At noon they passed the Prairie Butes, which are a collection of isolated hills, rising from the level plain, as if out of the sea. As they were visited by the party that passed through from Oregon, I shall give a particular account of them in the narrative of that journey. They formed one of the connecting links between the operations of the two parties, and served to verify their respective observations. Indians were seen on the west bank of the river, with a number of women in company, who seemed well disposed to enter into communication, as they motioned the party to land.

In the afternoon they encamped on the west bank, at a considerable distance above the Butes. The river was here only two hundred feet wide, and its banks but fifteen feet high. The trees on the shores had now become quite thick, and grew with great luxuriance; so much so, that were the sight confined to the river banks, it might be supposed that the country was one continued forest, instead of an open prairie.

The Indians who visited them at this camp, were less timid, and a much finer-looking set of men than those before seen. They allowed the officers and men to examine their bows and arrows, and appeared to have confidence in our good feeling towards them. The old chief welcomed the party, granted them permission to encamp on the bank, and then departing with all his tribe, nothing more was seen of him until late the next morning.

On the 31st, they again proceeded, and passed several Indian villages. Before noon, they arrived at a substantially-built fish-weir, of which the Indians began to take a part down, but Lieutenant-Commandant

Ringgold deeming that this was the termination of his exploration, motioned to them to desist. This fish-weir was constructed with a great deal of art: stakes, pointing down the stream, had been driven into its bed, having three openings, which led into square pens above; over each of the entrances into the pens was a platform, on which the natives stand to take the fish; on these also there were heaps of ashes, indicating that the natives make use of fire to attract the fish. The annexed wood-cut is a representation of the weir.

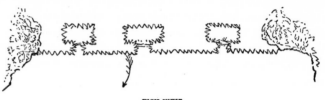

FISH-WEIR.

The river was examined for two or three miles above, and found to be filled with rapids, and innumerable difficulties caused by snags and sand-bars. Here Lieutenant-Commandant Ringgold ascertained his position to be in latitude 39° 13′ 39″ N., longitude 122° 12′ 17″ W., which, joined to the work of the land party, gives the exploration of the whole extent of the Sacramento river, from its source to the sea, a distance of two hundred miles. The first fork, or the junction of Pitt's with that of Destruction river or creek, is in latitude 40° 47′ N., longitude 122° 34′ W.

The Indians of this tribe, the Kinkla, were disposed to be much more friendly than those met with during the two preceding days. The party had some intercourse with them, and many of the women were seen, some of whom wore the peculiar Polynesian dress, called the maro, which in this case was made of strings from the California flax, which is common in this part of the country. Where this cannot be procured, they use the tula. This garment hangs in considerable thickness both before and behind, but is open at the sides.

Of these Indians it is reported that no one has more than one wife. Their village was similar to that already described. The women were not very prepossessing in their appearance, although the younger ones had pleasing faces and fine forms; but the men were large and stout, and would be termed finely formed. The women were employed in drying grass-seed and acorns in the sun, of which the latter seemed to be the principal part of their food. These Indians had small fishing-nets, somewhat resembling in size and shape a lady's reticule. These they made use of when diving for mussels, and in a short time procured half a bushel of them. They had also larger nets, which very much resemble our own; but on close examination, the manner of forming strands of the cordage was found to be different.

Their language is soft compared to that of the northern Indians, and as much so as that of the Polynesians. In but a few cases was the guttural sound of *tch* observed; and the repetition of syllables is frequent, as "wai-wai," and "hau-hau-hau." Lieutenant-Commandant Ringgold obtained a small vocabulary of the language from a chief, and Captain Suter furnished much information respecting it. According to him, although there are many tribes, yet they speak no more than two distinct languages, one of which prevails on the east and the other on the west side of the Sacramento. This information, however, was contradicted by other authorities; but as this subject belongs to the report on philology, I must refer the reader to Mr. Hale's book on that subject for further information.

According to the best authorities, these Indians, so far from being cannibals, will not eat any kind of animals that eat man. They carry burdens in the same manner as the northern tribes, with a strap around the forehead. They live upon various plants, in their several seasons, besides grapes, and even use the Artemisia. A species of tobacco is found on the sandy beaches, which the Indians prepare and smoke.

Their bows and arrows were carefully made, and the latter were kept in quivers made of fox-skins, young bears, &c. In each of these they had about forty arrows, pointed with flint and neatly made.

The vegetation throughout the whole course of the Sacramento showed evident traces of salt, and in some places the prairies seemed to be incrusted with it.

At the place where the survey ended, the river was two hundred feet wide, its banks being twenty feet above the river; but it was evident that its perpendicular rise exceeded this, as there was every appearance of its overflowing them; and, according to the testimony of the Indians, the whole country was annually inundated.

On the afternoon of the 31st of August, the party turned to go down the stream, and with thhe aid of the current made rapid progress. Towards sunset they entered the small stream called Bute, on whose banks they encamped. Here they were much disturbed, both with bears and musquitoes.

On the 1st of September, they made an early start, and about noon reached the village where the theft of Dr. Pickering's pistol had been committed.

It was with some difficulty that the Indians were persuaded to approach; but a fine-looking savage, more bold than the rest, at last ventured to do so, and gave the information that the Indian who had committed the theft, resided at the village up stream.

The weapon therefore not being forthcoming, Lieutenant-Commandant Ringgold determined to seize this man as a hostage for the return of the article. He was accordingly secured, his arms pinioned behind him, and led down to the boat, when two men were ordered to tie his legs; while they were in the act of doing this, he extricated himself, and jumped overboard. The guns were at once levelled, and half a dozen triggers ready to be pulled; but Lieutenant-Commandant Ringgold very properly stopped them from firing, and endeavors were made to recapture him, but without effect. These efforts having failed, they took to their boats, and pulled down the stream. The Indians who were on the banks, to the number of two hundred and fifty, made no demonstrations of hostility.

Platforms similar to those erected by the Indians for spearing salmon, were passed along the river banks.

Having stopped at the same camp at the Poplar Grove, as on the 28th, they took a few hours' amusement in hunting. Each person who went out returned with an elk or a buck as a prize, with large antlers. According to the hunters, the elk obtains an additional prong every year; and one of those killed had sixteen. The antlers are shed every year, and only acquire hardness at the rutting season, when the velvet is rubbed off. The usual length of their life is from eight to ten years.

On the 3d, they continued the survey, until they were below Feather river, when the provisions were so nearly exhausted that Lieutenant-Commandant Ringgold found that it would be impossible for him to examine that stream. The residents and trappers informed me that they had followed it to its source. From them I learned that it takes its rise in the Californian Range, from which it pursues a southwest course, until it falls into the Sacramento river. It is about forty miles in length. It is believed that the Spaniards, when they first explored this country, designated the Feather river as the Sacramento, and gave to the true Sacramento the name of the Jesu Maria. In no other way, at least, can the error which has occurred, in relation to the Jesu Maria, be explained; and on this supposition, the accounts of it become intelligible.

In the neighbourhood of the Sacramento, there are sometimes to be found small lakes or bayous, which seem to be filled at high water, but become stagnant during the dry season. These the elk and deer frequent in large numbers. Their cry or whistle is at times very shrill, and may be heard for a great distance.

At the junction of the Feather river with the Sacramento, the latter increases in width to nearly double. It was found just below the junction to be from twelve to fifteen hundred feet broad, forming a sort of bay, but it soon again contracts. They encamped about ten miles below the confluence of these streams.

Whilst the men were employed in pitching the tents, Dr. Pickering strolled up the bank, to see what he could find in the botanical way, without arms. On his approaching the bushes, a huge grisly bear made for him, and so close was he that it was necessary for him to make all the exertion he could to effect his escape from so dangerous an adversary. He gave the alarm, and every one was running for his arms, but before these could be prepared, this inhabitant of the forest made a precipitate retreat, and was soon beyond the reach of the rifle.

On the 4th, they had returned to Captain Suter, where they found that a small Russian schooner had arrived from Bodega, bringing the governor of that establishment, who was about delivering it up to Captain Suter. The vessel was understood to have been built at Sitka, and was of only thirty tons burden, very much resembling an English vessel of the same class.

For a boat they use a skin "badaka," that is admirably adapted for the seas and weather they have to contend with. When the persons are seated, and the opening closed, with a skin dress they more resemble an aquatic animal than any thing else.

The morning after their arrival, Captain Suter paid his men their weekly wages, in cloths, calicoes, vests, shirts, and pantaloons. The whole was arranged through their chief, who spoke a little Spanish. The labourers are obtained from the different rancherias, and some from the vicinity of the mountains. It was observed that the larger portion of the labourers were young men and boys; no women were employed, and as yet their services are not needed; but it is the Captain's intention, as he informed our gentlemen, to have employment for them in a year or two.

Several Americans from the United States are beginning to settle in this part of the country, and it will not be long before it becomes in some respects, an American Colony.

Although it was late in the season, a few salmon were caught at the fishery; they were not to be distinguished from the Columbia species of the first run.

The Indians have several rancherias around New Helvetia. Their lodges are all somewhat like low haycocks, being composed of a framework of sticks, thatched with the bulrush. In these there was no excavation, neither were they covered with earth; these dwellings were at the time deserted by the Indians, who were found encamped about a half mile nearer the river, with but a few boughs and mats to shelter them. The latter are manufactured after the manner that has been described as used by the Indians of Oregon.

At the rancheria, the men are generally found engaged in various games of chance, similar to those before described; it is not believed, however, that they carry their gambling propensities to such an extent as to stake their liberty. On the women, all the drudgery seems to be thrown. They were seen engaged in weaving water-tight baskets: these are very neatly made, of sufficient capacity to hold a bushel, and in these it is said they contrive to boil water and cook their food.

In the preparation of the acorn-bread all assist. The acorns are gathered in very large quantities, piled in heaps, and spread in the sun to dry. Both men and women are to be seen employed shelling, pounding, and baking them into bread: the pounding is performed upon a plank that has been hollowed out, with a stone pestle. To reduce the large quantity to a fine powder, requires great labour. This employment presents a busy scene, though the want of cleanliness, I may almost say pig-like filthiness with which it is performed, excites disgust.

INDIANS POUNDING ACORNS.

Around New Helvetia, although but a few days had elapsed since their former visit, the country, if possible, appeared more arid; it by no means justified the high encomiums that we had heard bestowed upon this far-famed valley. Our expectations probably had been so much raised as scarcely to allow us to give it that credit it really deserves.

The valley of the Sacramento may include a space of one hundred and eighty miles long, by from twenty to fifty miles wide. A large part of this is undoubtedly barren and unproductive, and must for ever remain so. The part that is deemed good soil, is inundated annually, not for any great length of time, yet sufficiently long to make it unfit for advantageous settlement. The high prairie is spoken of as being in general barren, and as affording but little good pasture.

The crops are usually ripe in June, which enables the wheat and Indian corn to be gathered before the summer drought begins. There is usually a rainy season of three months, but during the year of our visit no rain had fallen; and from every crop having failed, the inhabitants had been living upon their cattle. The cattle suffered almost as much as the crops, and large numbers of them died from starvation. On this account, the inhabitants had forborne to kill their cattle for hides, believing it to be a great loss to do so, as the weight was so much depreciated as to pay little more than the labour of slaughter and preparing for market.

The variety of game in this country almost exceeds belief. The elk may be said to predominate, but thre are also many bears, black-tailed deer, wolves, foxes, minxs, hares, musk-rats, badgers, antelopes, and Ovis montana. The wolf is reported by Dr. Marsh to be the same as the prairie-wolf of the Upper Mississippi, but not the one described by Say. Mr. Peale in his report will probably assimilate it to the small one of Oregon, with large ears. The fox is the same as the gray one of the wooded parts of the United States. According to Mr. Peale, the black-tailed deer is the only species found in this country. The Ovis montana has been frequently seen by Dr. Marsh; its coating is altogether hair, without any admixture of wool. No specimens were obtained for the Expedition.

The badger was seen by Dr. Pickering, who attempted to capture one, he found no difficulty in following it, as its movements were not very rapid. After passing over some hills, it made a stand; and as he approached, bristled up, but made no other threatening demonstration, and retreated backwards to its burrow. On his feigning a retreat, it came again forth and exposed itself to be fired at. Dr. Pickering wounded it; but not so much as to prevent its reaching its burrow, and so it escaped. He was satisfied by its movements, that its curiosity was the cause that led it to risk destruction. This seems to be the great and all-powerful instinctive passion of these wild animals, and frequently retains them within reach of the deadly rifle. Considering the quantity of game, the success attendant on our tyro hunters was not equal to their anticipations, and convinced them that it is much easier to bring down an elk in anticipation than in reality. The accidents were few, and only one annoyance was experienced, in the chase of a skunk, which obliged the officer to part with his clothes. The wild-fowl scarcely claimed attention, the elk and large animals being so abundant. The flesh of the elk was much preferred by the party to that of the deer.

On the 6th, the survey being finished down to this point, they descended the river, on their return to the ship. On the 8th, they had arrived at the mouth of the river, and the Straits of Kaquines. On the 9th, at midnight, they reached the Vincennes, after an absence of twenty days. Subsequent to this date, on the 20th, Lieutenant-Commandant Ringgold proceeded again, with six boats, to examine the bay of San Pablo, and the streams that flow into it, and also up the San Joachim, until it branched off to the southward and eastward. This party returned to the ship on the 29th.

Whilst the Vincennes was at Sausalito, the officers made visits to the different places around, and received many persons on board, priests as well as laymen; and as their estancias or mission-houses were far removed, they became guests for a longer time than was agreeable to most of the officers. A Californian needs no pressing to stay, as long as he is pleased with the place; and that he should be so, it is not necessary to furnish him with luxuries: he is content with coarse fare, provided he can get enough of strong drink to minister to his thirst. I have already spoken of the great consumption of spirits that is said to take place in this country; and from the experience we had of it, the accounts certainly are not exaggerated. The palm for intemperance was, I think, generally given to the padres, some of whom, notwithstanding their clerical robes, did ample justice to every drinkable offered them; and so well were they pleased, that some of them made a visit of three days' duration, and were even then disinclined to leave. It is not to be denied that they left the same impression of their characters on board that it has been heretofore said they bear on shore. The officers all seemed disposed to draw a veil over the conduct to which they were witnesses, and I will not be the one to raise it, as it can be of little benefit, and might perhaps be applicable to only a few of the order.

Our intercourse with Señor Martinez and his family was much

more agreeable. Of them, Captain Beechey has given a delightful account. Martinez has now retired to an estancia, where he is living in what is, in this country, affluence. His wife and himself have grown older, but still retain the character drawn of them by Captain Beechey. Near Pinole, Señor Martinez has a large house, but meagerly furnished, where he is surrounded by his large family of children and grandchildren. His wife is the same managing body, and keeps a strict eye upon her younger daughters, who are all good-looking.

The Californians are always inclined for amusement, and dancing is their favourite pastime, so that where a family is large, they seldom fail to pass off the evening pleasantly for their guests. Quadrilles and Spanish dances are the fashion; and the desire to please is as strongly exhibited in this family as it was during the visit of Captain Beechey. After dancing until a late hour, supper was provided, when the guests were either accommodated for the night, or set out to return to their homes, which, if they be unable to reach, they pass the night in the open air, using their ponchos and saddle-cloths for covering. During the nights there is but little wind, and the atmosphere is generally so dry and clear, that a person may, with impunity, sleep in the open air.

Three of the daughters and two of the sons of Señor Martinez are married; one of the former to Don Vitro Castro, and another to the captain of the port, an Englishman by the name of Richardson, who lives at Sausalito, and who supplies vessels with provisions. He was very attentive and obliging in furnishing the ship with supplies, and affording us the means of baking bread for the daily supply of the ship.

Captain Richardson has an estancia, bordering on Sausalito Bay, prettily situated under the hill, with sufficient fertile land for his gardens, or rather fields, where his vegetables are raised. His house is small, consisting of only two rooms, and within a few rods of it all the cattle are slaughtered, which affords a sight and smell that are not the most agreeable. A collection of leg-bones, hoofs, horns, and hides, lay about in confusion, for which numerous dogs were fighting. It was with great difficulty that these animals could be made to cease their strife; and what with this and the barking kept up by others, both without and within doors, there was such a clamour raised as required all the household, consisting of husband, wife, daughter, and slave, to quiet. Captain Richardson's establishment is a fair representation of the manner of living in California, and articles which are condemned elsewhere are acceptable here. However small the apartment may be, it is but sparingly furnished, and with no view of comfort, in our sense of the word; cleanliness, the great promoter of it, is wanting, and the indolence of the people seems an insuperable bar to it. Señora Richardson shows the marks of former beauty, which her daughter has inherited, and is said to be the handsomest woman in all California. I had the honour of seeing them when I returned Captain Richardson's call, and they were, in the Spanish style of beauty, quite deserving of the reputation they had acquired.

Captain Richardson did what he could to afford amusement for the officers, and during the visit of Señor Martinez to the ship, an invitation to a dance was accepted by some of them. Although the house was small, yet they made out to pass the evening with great hilarity, Señor Martinez dancing with two of his granddaughters—one on each arm. The group of musicians it was thought might have sat for the portraits of Roman soldiers. The evening's entertainment passed off well, the dancing having continued the greater part of the night. The Californians must be ranked next to the Chilenos for their love of this amusement. The refreshment consisted principally of strong drinks. Señor Martinez is looked upon as one of the aristocrats of the country. Much deference is paid to his opinion, and an alliance with his family is much sought after. The old lady exercises a matronly care over her daughters, and has them ever under her watchful eye. Captain Richardson's daughter, though only seventeen, is so famed for her beauty and attractions, that she has several avowed suitors. Courtships are here conducted somewhat in an old-fashioned manner. The suitor is obliged to avow himself and receive permission to visit. All who visit the estancia near Pinole will meet with that warm reception and kind treatment that Señor Martinez, his lady, and family, are so remarkable for.

On the opposite side of the bay of San Pablo, or to the west, are some of the finest tracts of country in California. One of these is called the Valley of Nappa, another that of Zonoma, and a third, San Rafael. In Zonoma is situated the town of the same name, the residence of General Vallejo, and the mission of San Rafael. The fertile country extends across to Ross and Bodega, the two Russian settlements before spoken of. Zonomo is the seat of government, and is situated in an extensive plain, with some high hills for its southern boundary. The plain is covered with fine oaks, and there is a never-failing stream of water passing through it. There is besides an inlet from the bay, which allows a boat navigation to it of about twelve miles.

Upon paper, Zonoma is a large city, and laid out according to the most approved plan. In reality, however, it consists of only the following buildings: General Vallejo's house, built of adobes, of two stories,

Drawn by A. T. Agate.

SHASTE PEAK.

Engraved by G. B. Ellis.

which fronts on the public square, and is said to be one of the best houses in California. On the right of this is the residence of the general's brother, Salvadore, and to the left, the barracks for the accommodation of the guard for the general, consisting of about twenty fusileers. Not far removed is the old dilapidated mission-house of San Francisco Solano, scarcely tenantable, though a small part of it is inhabited still by the Padre Kihas, who continues, notwithstanding the poverty of his mission, to entertain the stranger, and show him all the hospitality he can.

Besides the buildings just enumerated, there were in the course of construction, in 1841, a neat little chapel, and a small building for a billiard-room. There are also three or four more houses and huts which are tenanted; and at some future day it may boast of some farther additions.

General Vallejo was one of those who figured in the revolution of 1836, and was then appointed Commandant-General of Alta-California. He is now the owner of large estates; and having chosen this part of the country for his residence, he is free from the opposition and broils that are continually growing out of the petty concerns of the custom-house and its duties. He is not over-scrupulous in demanding duties of the vessels entering the port of San Francisco; and until he has been seen and consulted, a vessel trading here is liable to an indefinite amount of duties. A portion of the payment adds to his wealth, and how much goes to the government is not known; enough, I was told, in some cases, to save appearances, and no more. The foreigners who trade here are very attentive to him; and it might be supposed, before making inquiry into the cause, that he is a great favourite with them. The highest official protection is necessary for all those who wish to prosper in their trade to this port, and to prevent exactions from subordinates.

I have already spoken of the unceremonious manner in which Captain Suter officiated as administrador of the district to the east of the Sacramento. The anecdotes related to me of Vallejo, in like manner, show a striking disregard for the lives, as well as for the property and liberty of the Indians and gente de razon. He is supreme, and acts with the same impunity as all his predecessors, with one or two exceptions, have done before him. As an instance of the lawless acts of the governors, it is said that one of them entertained the idea of training the Indians as soldiers, and a company of them had been brought together, drilled, and made such proficiency in the use of their arms, that his excellency became alarmed, and forthwith ordered them all to be shot! I have little doubt that this story may be essentially true, for the value of an Indian's life in the eye of the rulers scarcely exceeds that of one of the wild cattle. The commandant-general is frequently said to hunt them, and by his prowess in these expeditions he has gained some reputation. Salvadore Vallejo is engaged in agricultural pursuits, and particularly in raising cattle, which, under the governor, he has the especial privilege of supplying to vessels, which he does at prices that insure a handsome profit. In times of scarcity, vessels are sure to be supplied by applying to the governor, who will order supplies to be furnished, and even obtain them by compulsion. On my arrival, finding that we wanted supplies, and not knowing how long (in the event of an accident to our land party) I might be detained, I was advised to apply to the commandant-general, through whom I would be sure of obtaining them. I therefore despatched a note by an officer, whom the general treated with great politeness, and returned for answer, that he could supply me with the following articles: Lima beans, wheat, potatoes, and other vegetables, which we had been unable to obtain. Fortunately for us, as well as for the lower orders and Indians, the party arrived, and we were not under the necessity of making use of his powerful intervention. The general, I was told, considers every bushel of grain as much at his command as he does the persons of the people, and the property of the state. Zonoma is to be the capital of this country, provided the general has power and lives long enough to build it up. An idea has got abroad that he is looking to the gubernatorial chair, and to be placed there by the same force that has raised Alvarado and himself to the posts they now occupy.

Zonoma is on the road that leads to Ross and Bodega; and by this route Captain Suter has transported all the stock he purchased of the Russians.

The reality of the hostility said to exist between these two rival administradors, seems doubtful, at least to the extent reported by the residents.

The state of society here is exceedingly loose: envy, hatred, and malice, predominate in almost every breast, and the people are wretched under their present rulers; female virtue, I regret to say, is also at a low ebb; and the coarse and lascivious dances which meet the plaudits of the lookers-on, show the degraded tone of manners that exists.

The mission of San Rafael is in the fertile valley of that name, about twelve miles from Sausalito, and consists of a large building, with a small chapel at its end; it is in a tolerable state of preservation, and is under the superintendence of an Irishman, named

Murphy. He has been put there, from its being considered a place of emolument, through his interest with the governor, and in order to pick up the crumbs that are still left. I understood, however, that Murphy had been disappointed in his expectations, and that it was his intention to establish himself elsewhere. Padre Kihas resides at this mission for six months of the year, and performs the duties of priest to those around it.

On the 24th of October, a fête was given at this place, in honour of the patron saint; and it was rumoured that there was to be a grand bull-fight. This spectacle came off accordingly, but was so miserably conducted as to prevent all kind of sport. The bulls had greatly the advantage, and the men and horses were tumbled about in a ridiculous manner, until they both became quite shy. They had cut off the tips of the bulls' horns, which was a fortunate circumstance for both horses and riders, who received no material injury. There was no bull and bear fight; in consequence, it was understood, of their not being able to procure one of the latter animals. In the fights between the bull and bear, it is said that however strong and savage the bull may be, the bear is always the conqueror: the only part of the bull he endeavours to attack is the tongue, by seizing which he invariably proves the victor.

When the fights were over, dancing was resorted to, and continued during the evening and all night. It was accompanied with hard drinking and uproarious conduct. Mr. Murphy's entertainment was considered fully equal to any that had been given for some time, and particularly the latter part of it, which may be better imagined than described.

Our duties at this port being completed, I felt desirous of knowing something of the missions at the south end of the bay of San Francisco, and, with Captain Hudson, determined to make a visit to them.

We left the Vincennes on the morning of the 29th, at an early hour, intending to reach the mission of Santa Clara by water. We stopped a short time at Yerba Buena to see Captain Hinckley and Mr. Spears, who kindly furnished us with a guide to point out the passages through the shoals, and the entrance to the creek that leads up to the Embarcadero, the landing whence the people of the mission usually ship their hides. We had a fine wind, and went briskly on until we reached the upper part of the bay, where we found our guide useless as a pilot. The consequence of his incapacity was, that we got on shore, and were detained so long that night overtook us before we entered the river Caravallio, that runs in a tortuous direction to the Embarcadero. Its course more resembled the turns of a corkscrew than any other thing to which I can liken it. I think we counted twenty-nine bends before we reached the point at which we were to disembark, which was nearly at the head of the creek. We were compelled to haul the boat along by the grass and rushes on each side, and it was near midnight before we achieved our object. As we passed through this narrow inlet, the birds that were lodged for the night, alarmed by the noise we made, flew in thousands from the marshes. Their fluttering was so great as to resemble the rushing of a vast wave; for as they rose, thousands seemed to follow thousands, until the sound died away in the distance, and again seemed to approach in an opposite direction. In the pitchy darkness, not a bird was to be seen, although they must have passed only a few feet above our heads.

At the Embarcadero we found no house or accommodations of any kind; but the guide soon led us to what he termed the road, which was found marked by the huge ruts made by the ox-carts. The walk was of service to us, as we had become chilled with the cold and damp air.

After proceeding a mile over a level plain, we reached the estancia. The first notice we had of it was a broken coural, and the ground covered with vast quantities of bones, hoofs, and horns. Over these we stumbled continually, until, on turning the corner of the coural, we were set upon by a pack of dogs, some fifty in number, which barked in every tone, from the snappish note of the pug to the sonorous voice of the bull-dog. All came forward, intent upon arresting our progress towards the large adobe building, which was now in dim outline before us. The bones served us as missiles to keep them at bay, and thus to protect our approach to the premises; and when we reached the porch, we gave the discourteous curs a full discharge. We knocked lustily for some time, but no answer was returned, nor could we see any light; but on a frequent repetition, each time redoubling our efforts, we at last heard light footsteps, and the door was suddenly opened by a little Indian girl, who ushered us into a large room, which, from the tables, chairs, and closets with china, we found to be the *salle à manger*. Here we had a full view of the interior; and the light which was burning in the adjacent rooms, showed us the occupants fast asleep. We had scarcely time to look around us, when a huge Californian, more than six feet in height, and proportionately large, stalked towards us in his shirt. His whole figure and countenance indicated a savage, and carried me back at once in idea to the Feejee cannibals. In a gruff tone he demanded our wants, and when he had satisfactorily ascertained who we were, and received a cigar as a token of friendship, he called up the whole family, consisting of a mother, two daughters, and several other children. These, after dressing themselves, came forth, and greeted us with genuine hospitality, with such pleasant faces and cheerful talk, that it was really delightful to find ourselves in such quarters; and our surprise was the greater, in consequence of the exterior having proved so uninviting. They immediately set about providing us with supper, consisting of tea, tortillas, valdivias, ollas, with eggs and a steak; and while this was in preparation by some, others were arranging the beds and changing the furniture of the sleeping-room. All this was done whilst the mother was talking and waiting upon us; and after supper was over, she pointed to our room, and then excused herself, by saying she must provide something for the sailors who had accompanied us; whilst we retired to rest, much fatigued with our jaunt.

The room was furnished differently from what we had been accustomed to, yet it was quite comfortable. The only piece of furniture that was not new to us was a high-post bedstead, evidently from our own country, though bedecked with old Spanish tapestry, in the way of tester, curtains, and valance. Instead of drawers, there were huge trunks, that put to shame those of modern construction. These contained the household linen and the finery of the females of the family, and were raised from the floor, that a broom might be passed underneath them. Here and there on the walls hung a new-made dress, of ample dimensions, and several Spanish sombreros, those that were of more recent date hanging highest; at least I judged them to be the best ones, from the careful manner in which they were covered up. There was no wash-stand; but a French ewer and basin, of the lozenge shape, of white and gold porcelain, were placed on a chair. A single looking-glass was hung high over it, its head inclining outwards. The dimensions of the frame were small, and the glass still smaller, owing to a figure of a patron saint occupying the larger part of the upper surface. Of chairs we had five, two with leathern seats and high backs; the others were of home manufacture. A large grated window, well barred with iron, with the thick and massive walls of an adobe house, gave it the look of security for confinement within, or against attack from without. Half a dozen coloured prints of the saints, ten inches square, in black frames, graced the walls.

Our beds, and every thing connected with them, were comfortable; and the manner in which we had been provided for made the entertainment doubly welcome. We found in the morning that we had occupied the sleeping-room of our hostess and her daughters, and that they had given it up expressly to accommodate us.

Before going to bed, we had made arrangements to send for horses to take us to the mission of Santa Clara, some three miles distant. None were to be obtained here, as the head of the family was now away, and had taken with him all those that were kept about the premises; the rest, we were told, were "muy lejos" (afar off).

The name of the family is Peralto, which is connected with the early settlement of California, and one of the most respectable in the country.

We arose about eight o'clock, and consequently missed our chocolate, which is given at an early hour, and could get no breakfast until eleven o'clock. Our horses had not arrived, and whilst we were waiting for them, Señor Don Miguel Felesfore de Pedrorena arrived from Yerba Buena, who at once made our acquaintance. He very kindly offered us his services to arrange matters, and to assist us on our way to Santa Clara, where he was then going. To this gentleman I feel myself much indebted. We found him a lively, intelligent companion, and well acquainted with the country and people. He is supercargo of several vessels on the coast, and extensively engaged in the peculiar manner of trading, of which I will have occasion to speak presently.

While horses were sought for us, we spent the time in looking around the premises. The house was a long one-story adobe building, with a thickly thatched roof, forming, by its projection, a piazza in front, supported by columns. There were many enclosures about the house, that gave it the appearance of a farm-yard and slaughter-house combined. Bones, hoofs, horns, and pieces of hide, were lying in every direction, and the ground was indented with the feet of cattle. Ducks, dogs, and fowls, were picking at the bones and offal. There were one or two ox-carts, of clumsy proportions, a bee-hive, and a lay-vat, formed of hide and suspended to four stakes, in the shape of a large bag, hung near by. At a short distance from the house was the vegetable-garden, where every thing grew in profusion, although without care. The only trouble in gardening was to put the seed into the ground, and await the result. This estancia is situated between two copses of wood, that grow on the banks of the brook that winds past it, and nearly join in the rear. In front is a plain, extending fifteen or twenty miles to the foot of the Sierra, which forms a pleasing and bold contrast to the flat surface, on which nothing is seen but here and there a small group of cattle, and immense flocks of wild geese; or some shrub, which, owing to the refraction, appears almost detached from the surface, and with dimensions so much enlarged as to appear like a great tree. The plain at this time was of a dark hue, somewhat resembling a light bronze colour, in consequence of the vegetation having been scorched up for many months.

About nine o'clock, five horses arrived instead of the eight we were in need of. These were literally the lame, halt, and blind, having sore backs, and being withal half starved. One had an eye protruding from its socket, another was without a tail. In any other country and place we should have refused to mount such horses; they were indeed sorry beasts, and compared with that of Don Miguel's, that had been in waiting for him, truly deplorable. Of the caparisons I shall only say, that sheep-skin and raw-hide predominated, although I regretted before the league was passed over that I had not had more of the former under me. I felt ashamed, even in California, to be thus mounted. We took leave of our kind hostess with many thanks for the attention she had showed us, and engaged her to provide an ample supply for the boats' crews during our absence.

The league between the Embarcadero and Santa Clara occupied us somewhat over an hour, for it was unbearable to attempt to ride faster than a walk. After ten o'clock, we came in sight of the mission of Santa Clara, and as we approached it the little ponds and damp places on the prairie were literally covered with wild geese, which would but barely open a way for us to pass through. They were far more tame than any barn-door geese I ever saw, and I could not easily divest myself of the idea that they were not domesticated.

The mission of Santa Clara has, at a distance, a respectable appearance; but on our drawing near the long line of huts, formerly occupied by the Indians, which are now destroyed, excepting a few, the ruin and neglect that have taken place are evident enough. The church and mission-house adjoining have also a dilapidated look; their tile roofs and whitewashed walls require extensive repairs, as well as all the wood-work of the doors, posts, &c. The church flanks the mission-house on the north, and is about one hundred and fifty feet long by forty wide, and about fifty feet high; it is surmounted by a small steeple. The mission-house is of only one story, with a corridor extending its whole length, of one hundred and fifty feet. This dwelling is now occupied both by the administrador and the padre, and a wall divides the premises into two parts, separating the temporal from the spiritual concerns of the establishment. The padre has his own servants, cooks, &c.

As we rode up with Don Miguel, we had no need of further introduction, and shared the kind welcome he received, as an old acquaintance, who had evidently much to do with the affairs of the mission, in the way of business. The administrador and his deputy came forth to greet us, with an ample retinue of attendants, of many varieties of colour, from the darkest Indian to the pure white. The administrador is a kind, excellent old man, who has risen from being a corporal in the army, to his present post. I could not learn his original name. His wife belongs to one of the best families in the country; and on her marriage with the administrador, she insisted upon his taking her name, which is Aliza, one of the most distinguished in California in bygone days. This, I understood, was not unusual, as the old family pride still predominates among these people. To the old lady we were soon introduced; her countenance and appearance bespoke her excellent character, which is well known throughout California. Nothing could be cleaner or more tidy than her house. Señor Aliza was too unwell to attend upon us, but his deputy acted as a substitute for that purpose. Shortly after our arrival, breakfast was announced, of which, after the ride we had had on our hard horses, we gladly partook.

This meal was considered by us as rather a light one, and consisted principally of fruit, and small ollas, peppers, &c. What it lacked in quantity was made up in quality. This was according to the usage of the country, and although Don Miguel wished to speak to Señora Aliza, with reference to a larger supply, we refused to give her any more trouble than could be avoided. She had prepared the whole with her own hands, and prided herself on her admirable management and cookery. Few certainly could equal her in the preparation of stews and delicate high-flavoured dishes; but of each there was a mouthful, and the deputy took good care to have more than his fair proportion. After breakfast, I strolled around the premises, and saw our good hostess busily engaged in directing her domestic concerns. The rear of the mission forms a quadrangle of low sheds, in which the domestic manufacture of candles, preserves, baking, and a variety of other duties, are performed. In these were some ten or fifteen Indians busily employed, and although clean, they did not excel so much in this respect as the interior of the main building, which appeared to be entirely under her own keeping.

Don Miguel proposed to us to make a visit to Padre Mercador, and that he might not be taken by surprise, a messenger was sent to ask at what hour he would be ready to receive us. This ceremony is deemed necessary, for the duties of the padre are considered here to be of such a nature as to preclude intrusion. Our messenger speedily returned with an intimation that he would be glad to have us pay him our visit at once. We were soon ushered into the small study of Padre Mercador, who received us with much courtesy. He is of the Franciscan order, good-looking, portly, and possesses a cheerful and intelligent countenance. Having Don Miguel to interpret in Spanish, and the padre speaking a little French, we made out to converse very well. His study is small, but contains many works of the old fathers, with several French authors, and comprises some six or seven hundred volumes. He showed us the different returns from the missions prior to 1828, but no attention had been paid since that date to the preservation of statistics. In Appendix VII., I have inserted one, in which the state of all the missions throughout Upper California is given, and which embraces not only their population but also the quantity of produce raised. This table will give an idea also of the management of the directors of the missions before the revolution. Since 1828, as already stated, the missions have been on the decline, and no returns have been given in, as was formerly required.

The padre spoke with resignation in relation to the manner in which the missions had been despoiled, and did not express any surprise that such things should have happened under their present rulers.

Padre Mercador served us with wine and fruit; of the latter, the pears were delicious. Don Miguel having notified me that it was expected our party should ask to see the church, I made the request; and the padre having supplied himself with a large bunch of keys, ushered us through several narrow passages, to the door of the vestry-room in the rear, into which we entered. Several pairs of massive candlesticks of silver were standing about on tables, and around the room were large trunks, which he opened, and showed us the rich altar-pieces, costly robes, and fine laces, which they contained. Many of the former were most magnificently embroidered in gold and silver, and composed of substantial silks and satins of divers colours. The splendour of the wardrobe was out of character with the smallness of the church; and on my remarking it, he said these things were for processions, to have effect upon "los gentiles." One or two small pictures that hung in this room were worthy of notice. Don Miguel asserted that he thought if I desired them, there would be no great difficulty in procuring any article that could be spared. I had no disposition to authorize him to make the attempt; but this suggestion tends to show in how little regard the obliging padre was held by the community. We next passed into the church, the whole length of which was thrown into one, without any columns. At one end is the altar, and at the other the choir, which the padre informed me con-

sisted of some eighty Indians, who are daily in practice. He said that
the Indians were fond of music, had good ears, and little difficulty was
found in teaching it to them. In making the selections of performers,
they generally took those whose physical qualifications seemed best
adapted to the particular instrument, and practice did the rest. In
this way, such music as pleased the Indians and people of the country,
and which therefore answered his purposes, was produced. The chapel
is painted in fresco, or I should rather say daubed, by a young artist
of Mexico. The saints are all represented in full costume, and the
scenes depicted are those most likely to attract the attention and wonder
of the neophytes. The whole has a gaudy and unsightly appearance.
We parted from Padre Mercador at the church door, knowing it was
about the hour of his noon service; and received from him a pressing
invitation to visit him in the evening, to play a game of chess, of which
he said he was very fond.

We now returned to the administrador, whom we found enveloped
in his large overcoat, with a white nightcap on his head, waiting in
his salle à manger to receive us, and afford us entertainment. Don
Miguel gave us the secret of this movement, saying, that his wife,
after our arrival in the morning, had persuaded him to go to bed; but
he could not resist the opportunity that now offered itself, of telling his
old stories over again to willing listeners; and we had scarcely taken
our seats, before he began a full account of his birth, parentage, &c.,
and was about relating his adventures in full, when the bell tolled noon.
He immediately sprang upon his feet, faced the south, and began to
cross himself, and repeat a prayer with great volubility. In this exercise he continued for a few minutes, until he heard the last taps of
the bell. Of this we took advantage to break up his discourse; which,
notwithstanding sundry efforts on his part, we succeeded in doing, and
it was not long before we heard he was again in bed. His deputy
answered all our questions, and assured me that he was well acquainted
with the concerns of the mission, for he had heard them very often
repeated by the administrador during the last few years.

The deputy now conducted us through the garden, which is surrounded by a high adobe wall, and has a gate that is always kept
locked. It was from one and a half to two acres in extent, and mostly
planted with grapes, which are cultivated after the Spanish fashion,
without trellises: some of the fruit was yet hanging, and was generally
of the sweet Malaga kind. Our guide informed me that the mission
took the first picking, for the manufacture of wine and to preserve,
then the inhabitants, the women of the "gente de razon," and afterwards the children. Strict watch was, however, kept that they did

not pull the other fruit. Only a certain number are allowed to work in the garden, and the whole is placed under the constant superintendence of a gardener. It would be almost impossible to protect the fruit otherwise. They have fruit of all kinds, both of the tropical and temperate climate, which they represented as succeeding admirably well. A few barrels of wine are made, but nothing can be more rude than their whole process of manufacturing it. The tillage is performed with ploughs that we should deem next to useless; they are nothing but a crooked piece of timber, four to six inches square, somewhat in the shape of our ploughs, which merely serves to loosen the ground to a depth of three or four inches; but in such a soil, and in this level land, this rude implement answers the purpose, and produces crops on an average of from sixty to eighty for one. The ploughs are drawn by oxen, and are well adapted to the Indians, who more readily learn to use them than they would more complicated machines.

After spending some time in the garden, we were recalled to dinner; and if we had cause to complain of the slightness of the breakfast, the dinner made ample amends, every variety of dish being abundant and admirably prepared. Don Miguel congratulated himself and us that the administrador was not in a fit state to prevent us from enjoying it, by the everlasting narration of his adventures. Señora Aliza had quite surpassed even her usual good feasts in this dinner, which called forth much praise from our companion.

At the missions throughout the country four meals are daily taken: at an early hour, chocolate; at eleven o'clock, breakfast; at two, dinner; and at seven, supper. The dinner and supper are the principal meals, and at them the Californians indulge to a great extent.

After our meal was finished, Don Miguel, having some business at the Pueblo of San Jose, about a league from Santa Clara, he invited us to accompany him thither. After some difficulty in procuring horses, we set out on sorry nags, and on leaving the mission entered an avenue lined on each side with large trees. These I understood had been planted at an early day, by one of the padres, in order to protect the people from the sun during the celebration of the church festivals, and to leave no excuse to the inhabitants of the pueblo for not visiting the mission church.

Just before arriving at the pueblo, we crossed over one of the tortuous branches of the Rio Guadaloupe, some twenty feet wide, and had a view of the pueblo. It seemed as if this were a gala-day, and as if every one were abroad celebrating it on the banks of this river, or rather creek; the overflow of which had served to keep the grass green for a considerable space around. Instead of its being a festival, it turned out to be the general washing-day of the village; and the long lines, trees, bushes, &c., were all hung with the many-coloured garments, which, with the crowds of men, women, and children, and some cattle, seen moving to and fro, or gathered in small groups, gave the whole quite a pleasing effect. I was told that the pueblo of San Jose had a larger number of inhabitants than any other in Upper California; but as we rode into it, it seemed almost deserted, and I would willingly have gone back and amused myself with the scene on the green, if Don Miguel had not represented to me, that his standing would be very much affected if we did not at once proceed to the alcalde's. We accordingly rode up to his house, a very pretty two-storied edifice, of a light-cream colour, in the centre of the main street, and directly opposite a new church that they are erecting. The alcalde gave us a cordial reception. His first appearance was that of a French pastry-cook, with his white cap and apron. He was a short, dapper, rosy-cheeked man, by birth a Frenchman, but had been now twenty years settled in the pueblo; was married, and had eleven children, who looked as healthy and as dirty as one would wish to see them. The moment he understood who his visitors were, he did us the honour to doff his white cap and apron; and shortly after appeared in a round-about, very much ornamented with braid, &c. The only name I heard him called by, was Don Pedro. He spoke his native language imperfectly, using a great many Spanish words with it, and told me that he had nearly forgotten it. From him I learned that the pueblo contained six hundred inhabitants, about forty of whom were whites. He described himself as the "sous-préfect," and said that he administered justice, inflicted punishment, and had the ability to make the inhabitants happy, as he thought they should be. On my asking, by what laws he administered justice, his answer was,—by what he thought right. He had very little trouble, except guarding against the attacks of the Indians and preventing them from stealing horses, of which he had great fears; he had, therefore, provided for the safety of his own by keeping them in a small shed attached to his house, and within a locked gate.

He considered the pueblo as in danger of attacks from the Indians, who were now in great numbers within striking distance, and had become very troublesome of late in driving off horses, of which they had lost three or four hundred, and he said that pursuit was impossible, as they now had no troops. I was not satisfied that the alcalde was the bravest man in the world, or that he thought much of the interests of those over whom he had sway. Don Miguel gave him the character of being a good customer, and generally punctual in his payments. He entertained us with wine and beer of his own making, and showed us the copy-books of his children, who were in pot-hooks and trammels, which he looked upon as a wonderful advancement in the education of the country. Some half-dozen books were all they owned in the pueblo; but to make up for this deficiency, the alcalde told me they were all very happy, and that there were but few quarrels, for those in which stabs were inflicted did not occur oftener than once a fortnight. We took our departure a short time before sunset, amidst the gathering in of the villagers, with their goods and chattels, to a place of safety. There are two Americans settled here, who own mills, but I was not fortunate enough to meet with them; the alcalde, however, gave them good characters. The evening was a beautiful one, and we had a delightful ride back to the mission; and our horses, knowing they were on their return, were quite mettlesome.

The mode of conducting business in this country is peculiar. Vessels, on reaching the coast, employ as a supercargo or travelling agent, some person well known throughout the country, who visits all the pueblos, missions, and estancias, as a traveller, passing from place to place without any apparent object of business. He thus has an opportunity of inspecting the worldly affairs of those to whom he desires to sell; and if he finds them apparently thrifty, he produces his card of patterns, and soon induces a disposition on the part of his host or hostess to buy, being careful to secure in payment as much of their worldly goods as he can, and trusting them for the rest of the indebtedness. A few live cattle delivered by each purchaser at the neighbouring pueblo, become by this means a large herd, which is committed to cattle-tenders on shares, who in due time slaughter them and deliver the hides. A large amount of goods is thus disposed of, to a very considerable profit. Large cargoes, consisting of a variety of articles, of both American and English manufacture, are thus sold. From the state of the country, it has been difficult to obtain payments or returns in money; but the debts have been paid in cattle, and probably will turn out well, when the rains return and allow the animals to be again slaughtered. When hides are given in payment, they are valued at two dollars, and are at all times the common currency of the country. No money is in circulation, unless what is paid out by the foreign merchants; and in lieu of change, an extra quantity of goods is taken, which excess is usually to the disadvantage of the buyer.

On our return to Santa Clara, we had to procure horses for our journey back by land. We had been told by the administrador and his deputy, that there would be no difficulty in the mission providing us with horses and saddles; and under this assurance, we had despatched our boats on their return to the ship, determining to make the ride of sixty miles the next day. We soon found that the mission horses were lame, and that they had strayed. These, with many other excuses, all showed us the dilemma we were in. Three or more messengers were pretended to be sent to the pueblo and the neighbouring estancias; and after much delay and several feigned disappointments, we were told that six animals might be procured. The exorbitant price of four dollars for each was asked for the use of these. A good horse may be purchased for eight dollars. As I at once saw the game that was in progress, I thought it better to comply with a good grace than perhaps suffer farther imposition; so six were agreed for at four dollars each, for the next day. I was well aware that the deputy was deeply in the plot, and probably shared a part of the profits.

Being disengaged in the evening, we went early to Padre Mercador's to play chess, for which he has more love than knowledge. He had boasted not a little of his prowess, but after suffering defeat in three successive games, his opinion of his skill was somewhat lessened. He was in fact but a novice in the game. For refreshments we had brandy and wine, with cigars and fruit, of which the hospitable padre and Don Miguel both partook most freely, particularly the former. We remained until nine o'clock, when a message was brought us that supper was ready, and we retired, leaving Padre Mercador to resume the duties of his office. For his kindness and attentions we were greatly indebted to him; I wish I could say that his mode of life and the influence he exerts over his charge, also deserved commendation.

At the head of the supper-table, we found Donna Aliza, with a huge dish of smoking valdivias before her, and a variety of edibles, with an infusion of tea in small cups, which, at the request of Don Miguel, was added to until it became drinkable, but not without many exclamations against its extravagance. The poor husband was in bed, and Captain Hudson, who went to see him, finding that he was suffering from a severe cold he had taken, prescribed bathing his feet, and a strong glass of hot whiskey punch. Don Miguel accordingly prepared the latter, which was cheerfully taken by the patient, who shortly afterwards fell into a sound sleep. In the morning, we found that he was entirely recovered.

Our beds were clean and comfortable, though the apartment had a strong smell of cordovan leather. The only place of deposit for clothing, &c., was, as we had seen in the estancia, in large trunks. The matin-bell aroused us at early dawn, when we heard the full choir practising. There was certainly nothing earthly in the sound, nor yet heavenly; much noise, but little music.

We were up betimes, but were threatened with disappointment in our horses. The kind and attentive Donna Aliza served us with chocolate and toast, and prepared cold tongues, chickens, and ample stores of bread for our use. At last the horses, together with the Indians who were to accompany us, made their appearance, and out of the number, I recognized at least three that belonged to the administrador, as I had been led to believe would be the case the evening before. His good wife ordered us their best saddles, but without the pillions or saddle-cloths.

After an hour's preparation, we took our leave and galloped off, in company with Don Miguel, who proposed to accompany us some six or seven miles, on our way to visit some of his herds, that were then feeding on the prairie. We had not proceeded far before we were overtaken by the person who had them in charge, coming at a furious gallop. He was mounted on the best horse I had seen in the country, and dressed after the Californian fashion, in a dark brown cloth jacket, thickly braided, both before and behind, with slashed sleeves, showing his shirt elegantly embroidered, both on the breast and sleeves; velvet breeches of bright blue, secured around his waist with a red sash, and open at the sides, ornamented with braid and brass bells, in abundance; below the knee he wore leather leggins, fastened with garters, worked in silver, and below these, shoes, over which were fastened large silver spurs, with the heavy rowels of the country; on his head was tied a red bandana handkerchief, and over that a huge broad-brimmed sombrero, with peaked crown, covered with an oil-silk cloth; the whole decorated with cords, aiguillettes, and ribands, with a guard-cord passing under the chin. His horse was equally well caparisoned, the bridle being decked with silver, as were the tips of his large wooden stirrups; with pillions and saddle-cloths in abundance. Few riders had so gay an air, or seemed to have so perfect a command of the animal he rode; and until we arrived at the wood where his Indians were looking out, he was an object of great attraction, assuming all the airs and graces of a person of high rank.

After galloping for several miles, we reached a few trees and bushes, that are designated as the "woods." Near by was a large herd of cattle feeding. The Rancheros we found lying about, in huts of hide, with a fire in front, and the leg-bone of an ox roasting over it; the skulls, bones, and offal, lay about, with hides here and there pegged to the ground.* Some score of dogs were disputing

* The hides of the cattle that die, or that are killed for food, are cured in this way.

over that last killed, and the ground around seemed alive with cranes, crows, &c., acting as scavengers, and disputing for their shares. There is no smell except that of raw beef; the climate is so dry that no putrid matter exists, but the sight is unpleasant enough to those who have not become accustomed to it.

Previous to setting out, we provided our saddles with extra sheep-skins; we now took leave of Don Miguel, with many thanks for his attentions, and a hearty shake of the hand. We soon found that our horses began to fag from the effects of our bad riding, and the fatigued and wretched condition they were in; and by the time we arrived at Las Pulgas, we found it necessary to change, and were glad to have a temporary relief from our saddles. Any one who has ever ridden upon a Californian saddle, with but a slender covering to it, will be able to understand our feelings. We were besides but ill provided for the trip, which our nags seemed not slow to discover. We had no well-armed heels, and were, besides, deficient in whips, both indispensable to a rider in California. The consequence was, that they could not be made to move along, without most laborious efforts of bodily strength.

The country we passed through was at this time destitute of both water and grass, and the weather uncomfortably warm. In places we found it picturesque, from the scattered oaks, laurels, &c., though to all appearance entirely unfit for cultivation. Wherever there was any running water, a pond, or vegetation, large flocks of geese and ducks were seen. At four o'clock, we entered the estancia of Señor Sanchez, to whom Don Miguel had given us a note of introduction, desiring that he would aid us if we wanted horses. We had looked forward to this point with hope, in the belief that our troubles in riding such forlorn beasts would terminate, and that our bodies as well as minds would be set at rest.

The word estancia seems to give one an idea of something more extensive than a small farm: it sounds more noble and wealthy; but whatever had been our opinion before, the reality disappointed us. Señor Sanchez's estancia at a distance was quite a respectable-looking building; the broad shadow cast by its projecting roof gave it a substantial and solid appearance; but a nearer approach dispelled these favourable impressions, and showed its uncouth proportions, as well as the neglect in which the whole was kept. The way to the house, which stands on a knoll, leads through miry places, and over broken-down fences, winding around dilapidated ox-carts, over troughs, old baskets, dead hogs, dogs, and fowls, all huddled together. Rude articles of husbandry occupied the sides of the building. Seeing no one,

Drawn by A. T. Agate.

J. W. Steel Sc.

ENCAMPMENT ON THE SACRAMENTO.

we dismounted, tied our horses, and began to search for inhabitants. All the houses were unfinished: to the doors of some there were no steps, and no floors to the rooms of others; the adobes were bare, and destitute of plaster or whitewash; and what was more disheartening, no inhabitants made their appearance. At last a slave was seen crawling from a wretched hole, whom we followed to the only place which yet remained unsearched, a distant corner of the premises, where we found the family, consisting of a mother and daughter. The latter was a nice-looking girl, to whom our note was handed, and who read it aloud to her mother, who did not recognise the name of Don Miguel. Whether this arose from design or ignorance, I know not; but the note produced no apparent effect: however, after a few compliments, and a little persuasion, through our servant, (who spoke Spanish well,) the mother was somewhat softened, and we procured a tumbler of milk and a tortilla; but we could not induce her to allow us to take from the fifty horses that were then in the coural, the few we required. Her constant answer was, that her husband was not at home, and she could not do it. We strayed about the kitchen, which was the only apartment fit for occupation, and warmed ourselves over the small fire that had been lighted, for the air was becoming chilly and damp. This apartment was lighted from the door and a small window; it was furnished with numerous stew-holes and ovens, which appeared very convenient for cooking; and above them were placed shelves, on which the pans of milk were resting. In the centre was a large mortar, and beyond it, at the far end, quite in the dark, the rude grist-mill of the country. To the long shaft of the mill a small donkey was harnessed. This place apparently answered also as a stable. The whole had quite a primitive look, and showed, at least, some comfort and forethought. During our examinations, in came the husband, very unexpectedly to his wife and daughter, as well as to ourselves. He had the face of a ruffian. After many suspicious looks and questions, he gave his consent, though very unwillingly, to supply us with horses. Lest it should be supposed that this man was the owner of the estancia, I must here say that Señor Sanchez was not at home; although I am not prepared to vouch, from what I heard afterwards, that our treatment at his hands would have been any better. We were told that it was but a short two hours' ride to Yerba Buena, and we hoped to reach it before dark. We therefore made haste to secure fresh horses, and soon took our departure. The horses were but sorry-looking animals, and I must own that the thanks for them were very difficult to utter.

We had scarcely gone beyond the "a dios" of our ill-looking friend, when the steed of Captain Hudson came to a stand, and no persuasion, whipping, or spurring, could induce him to move. It was then discovered that he was blind, and in attempting to move him we found he was lame also. My servant John was then directed to change, as he was the best horseman of the three, and after a trial of patience, succeeded in getting him along.

After dark we reached the house of Mr. Spears, at Yerba Buena. We were barely able to dismount, having had one of the roughest and most fatiguing rides I ever experienced. A warm welcome from our countryman at Yerba Buena, and a seat at his hospitable board, soon refreshed us. My boat being in waiting, we embarked, and reached the Vincennes at two o'clock in the morning, greatly fatigued, yet highly gratified with our jaunt to the mission of Santa Clara.

Finding all those belonging to Lieutenant Emmons's party had now joined the ship, preparations for sea were at once made. I shall now take up the operations in Southern Oregon, which will form the subject of the following chapter.

SACRAMENTO INDIANS GAMBLING.

CHAPTER III.

CONTENTS.

CHAPTER III.

SOUTHERN OREGON.

1 8 4 1.

he last chapter closed with the arrival of Lieutenant Emmons and his party at San Francisco. I shall now give some account of the operations of this party, and of the country they passed through. The difficulties which were experienced in the organization of the party, have already been alluded to in another place, and need not be repeated. There remain to be described some of the articles of his equipment, in the preparation of which much time was consumed, and which were absolutely necessary for the success of the expedition. The principal part of the provision was flour; this is packed in sacks; the sacks are again enclosed in a "parflesh" made of hide, to protect them from being torn to pieces by the boughs of trees and underwood; this rests upon a pack-saddle, by which the load is firmly secured on the horse; while, to protect his back from injury, a thick saddle-cloth called "appichemens" lies beneath the pack-saddle. These articles are represented in the annexed cut.

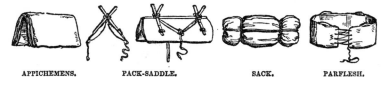

APPICHEMENS.   PACK-SADDLE.   SACK.   PARFLESH.

To these are to be added the trail-rope and lash-cord, six or eight fathoms in length. These trails drag on the ground, and are intended for the purpose of catching the horses. Now, all these articles were to be prepared in a country where no mechanic is to be found; and so indispensable are they, that any party which sets out without them would in all probability be compelled to return.

Our gentlemen, when they left Vancouver, proceeded by the way of the Hudson Bay Company's farm on Multunomah or Wapautoo Island, which is near the place where Captain Wyeth had erected his fort. They then crossed the river and went towards the Faulitz Plains, passing on their route a large grazing farm belonging to the Company, and those of many settlers. From these they were supplied with fresh horses. They found the country beautiful, and the land rich. Their route lay over hills and through prairies. The hills were wooded with large pines and a thick undergrowth of rose-bushes, Rubus, Dogwood, and Hazel. The prairies were covered with variegated flowers, and abounded in Nuttallia, Columbines, Larkspurs, and bulbous-rooted plants, which added to the beauty, as well as the novelty of the scenery.

Some sickness had made its appearance among the members of the party. Messrs. Emmons, Peale, Rich, and Agate, all had attacks of ague and fever, and the two last-named gentlemen suffered much from this disease. Dr. Whittle ascribed these attacks to the length of time, nearly five weeks, during which they had been encamped on the Willamette, and particularly to the position of the camp, immediately on the bank of the river, where it was subject to the damp and fogs.

When the party set out, new difficulties arose from the fact that the horses had for some time been unused to saddles or packs, and from the awkwardness of the riders. Corporal Hughes of the marines, one of the party, was thrown from his horse, which took fright at some wild animals crossing his path. The pack-horses were missing, and caused much difficulty in hunting them up; one, when found, had waded into a creek with pack and all, and stood there with only his head out of water. At this an old hunter became enraged, and springing into the water, thrust his thumb into the horse's eye; the pain of which treatment caused the animal to leap up the opposite bank with great agility, leaving part of his load behind. The part thus left proved to be the medicines prepared for the party; but these were recovered, and being in phials were not materially injured. On reaching the first encampment, Smith the marine and his horse were both missing: to guide him, guns were fired during the night; but he did not make his appearance. In the morning, parties were sent in search of him and the pack-animals. In the afternoon, the marine made his appearance, without any other loss than the ramrod of his musket; he had passed the night in the woods. This same man, a day or two after, reported to Lieutenant Emmons that he had lost his riding horse: he was very properly told to go in search of him, and if he could not find him, to return to Vancouver, as he was too helpless to be of any use. This had the desired effect, and from that day forth, he proved a useful man. There were many other annoyances and difficulties that Lieutenant Emmons's patience and perseverance overcame.

INDIAN BURIAL PLACE, OREGON.

During the time of their stay, Mr. Agate made many sketches. One of these is of a burying-place, which I have thought worth inserting, as exhibiting one of the peculiar features of a race which is now fast disappearing. The mode of burial seems to vary with almost every tribe: some place the dead above ground, while others bury their departed friends, surrounding the spot with a variety of utensils that had been used by the deceased.

The graves are covered with boards, in order to prevent the wolves from disinterring the bodies. The emblem of a squaw's grave is generally a cammass-root digger, made of a deer's horns, and fastened on the end of a stick.

From the delay of the party in the Willamette Valley, they became well acquainted with the various characters of the people who were settled there. They generally consist of those who have been hunters in the mountains, and were still full of the recklessness of that kind of life. Many of them, although they have taken farms and built log houses, cannot be classed among the permanent settlers, as they are ever ready to sell out and resume their old occupations, when an opportunity offers. Our party found them, with one or two exceptions, well disposed.

The gentlemen of the party, who had more time and opportunity to become acquainted with the operations of the missionaries than I had, were less favourably impressed than myself. One of the principal complaints of the settlers against the members of the mission was, that they never had any religious service, although several ministers of the mission were unemployed. This complaint, however, could not be made on our part; for, the first Sunday the party was encamped, the Rev. Mr. Leslie invited them all to his house for that purpose, which invitation was accepted. Tibbats, one of the party, was sitting by an open window during the sermon, and, as many have done before him, was nodding, in which motion he threw his head back and struck the stick that supported the sash, which coming down suddenly, caught him by the neck. This accident occasioned no small disturbance in the congregation, but no injury resulted from it to the man, who was inclined to join in the laugh that unavoidably took place after he was extricated. This anecdote will show the character of the class of settlers which the missionaries would have to deal with, and I am inclined to believe that for the neglect of duty imputed to them, those who make the charge are themselves chiefly to blame.

It was the general impression of our party, however, that the field for a mission was but small, and not sufficient to warrant the expenses that have been lavished upon it. Their school was in operation, and included twenty pupils in all. Dr. Babcock mentioned to one of our gentlemen that he had a native boy for a servant, of whose qualifications and education he spoke, saying that it was a great trouble to get him into cleanly habits, such as washing his face and hands in the morning, before he milked the cow. He next taught him to make a fire, boil a tea-kettle, and make tea; he then taught him to fry and bake; he could wash clothes, and would in a short time be able to iron.

All our gentlemen experienced the same kind treatment and good fare that I have before spoken of, and nothing seemed to be wanting in the way of substantial comforts.

The party, including Passed Midshipmen Eld and Colvocoressis, Messrs. Dana, Brackenridge, and the sergeant, proceeded up the Willamette river. They reached Champooing on the 3d, where they disembarked. In the morning they were taken to the house of Thomas M'Kay, who is one of the most noted persons in this valley, particularly among the mountain trappers. He is a man of middle age, tall, well-made, and of muscular frame, with an expression of energy and daring, and a deep-set, piercing black eye, beneath a full projecting eyebrow. Among the trappers he is the hero of many a tale, and is himself prone to indulge his guests with his personal adventures. He lives in a house that answers both for a dwelling and grist-mill, and is said to be the best belonging to a settler in the valley. This man was engaged to go as guide; and, what speaks little for his veracity and principles, at the last moment refused to do so, and afterwards made his boast that he had fooled the party, as he had not intended to go from the first. His harvest had just been reaped, which he said had produced him twenty-five bushels to the acre. M'Kay furnished them with horses, and accompanied the party to the camp, where they arrived early in the afternoon. Here all was preparation for a speedy departure, and every one fully occupied, with packs, saddles, and trappings. On the 7th, the party made their final move, and after travelling only six miles, encamped near Turner's, known as the mission butcher. He owns a farm, in the acceptation of the word in Oregon, having a log-hut, an Indian woman to reside in it, and an undefined quantity of land. The hut contains no furniture to sit or lie upon, and only the few articles most needed in cooking. He does not cultivate any thing, but supports himself by killing cattle semi-weekly. Report says that he was formerly a drummer in the United States service, but for upwards of thirteen years he has led the sort of life he now does. He seems both contented and independent, and appears an honest and good-natured fellow. He has had several narrow escapes, having been twice with parties that were attacked by the southern Indians, in the passage to and from California. The last time he was one of four who escaped, subsisted on berries and roots for a fortnight, and was obliged to travel only at night, to avoid the Indians who were in search of him. He furnished our party with fresh beef of his own stock, refusing to receive pay, and seemed very much incensed that the mission should have charged for what had been obtained from them.

The country in the southern part of the Willamette Valley, stretches out into wild prairie-ground, gradually rising in the distance into low undulating hills, which are destitute of trees, except scattered oaks;

these look more like orchards of fruit trees, planted by the hand of man, than groves of natural growth, and serve to relieve the eye from the yellow and scorched hue of the plains. The meanderings of the streams may be readily followed by the growth of trees on their banks as far as the eye can see.

They were detained here by the straying of their animals, and did not succeed in getting off until the next day, when Turner gave them two of his horses, being willing to run the risk of recovering the lost ones in their stead.

On the morning of the 9th, they had a severe frost. In the course of the day they passed Creole Creek, and encamped on the Ignas. The atmosphere during the day had become quite thick, owing to the smoke arising from the burning of the prairie. Here they prepared themselves fully for their journey, by trimming their horses' hoofs, and taking a full account of them. The soil was a red decomposed basalt, well adapted for grazing and wheat lands.

On the 10th, the country was somewhat more hilly than the day previous, but still fine grazing land. During the day they crossed many small creeks. The rocks had now changed from a basalt to a whitish clayey sandstone. The soil also varied with it to a grayish-brown, instead of the former chocolate-brown colour, which was thought to be an indication of inferior quality. The country had an uninviting look, from the fact that it had lately been overrun by fire, which had destroyed all the vegetation except the oak trees, which appeared not to be injured.

On the 11th, after passing during the day Lake Guardipii, which is about five hundred yards long, they encamped on the Lumtumbuff river, which is a branch of the Willamette. This river is a deep and turbid stream, branching out in places like a lake, but being in general narrow and fordable.

On the 12th, the route was across a parched-up prairie, some portions of which were composed of gravel and white sand, mixed with clay. The paths were very rough, owing to the soil, which was much cut up by the herds that had been driven through; and which, on becoming hard, was exceedingly fatiguing to the horses. Bands of wolves were met with, and were heard throughout the night howling in various parts of the prairies. The cry of these animals is peculiar: one sets up a long shrill whine, three or four join in, and in a few moments afterward, the whole pack utter a sort of sharp yelp, which gives the idea of a half-laughing, half-crying chorus. The party had hitherto made from fifteen to twenty miles a day; and in travelling this day, the animals suffered a great deal from want of water. They encamped on the Malé creek, which was about thirty feet wide, and ran in a northerly direction.

On the 13th, they had much difficulty in finding their horses, which had escaped the guards at night, owing to the thick fog that prevailed. They were in consequence unable to go forward until three o'clock in the afternoon; some of the animals had gone six miles back on the trail in search of water, and were found in the vicinity of marshy places. Messrs. Emmons and Eld had employed the hours of this detention in getting dip and intensity observations. In consequence of this mishap, they were unable to make more than two miles during the day, which continued hot and foggy.

Some wandering Callapuyas came to the camp, who proved to be acquaintances of Warfields' wife: they were very poorly provided with necessaries. Mr. Agate took a characteristic drawing of one of the old men.

COSTUME OF A CALLAPUYA INDIAN.

These Indians were known to many of the hunters, who manifested much pleasure at meeting with their old acquaintances, each vying with the other in affording them and their wives entertainment by sharing part of their provisions with them. This hospitality showed them in a pleasing light, and proved that both parties felt the utmost good-will towards each other. The Indians were for the most part clothed in deer-skins, with fox-skin caps, or cast-off clothing of the whites; their arms, except in the case of three or four, who had rifles, were bows and arrows, similar to those I have described as used at the north; their arrows were carried in a quiver made of seal-skin, which was suspended over the shoulders.

On the 15th, they reached the base of the Elk Mountains, which divide the valley of the Willamette from that of the Umpqua. The ascent and descent of this ridge are both gradual, and the hills were covered with pines, spruces, and oaks, with a thick undergrowth of Hazel, Arbutus, Rubus, and Cornus. Through these thickets they were obliged to force their way along the back of one of the spurs, and were three hours in reaching the top, which was fifteen hundred feet above the level of the plain. A species of Castanea was met with, whose leaves were lanceolate and very rusty beneath; the cup of the nut was very prickly.

The route over the Elk Mountain was very serpentine, owing to the obstruction caused by fallen timber, many of whose trunks were four and five feet in diameter. Previous to ascending the mountain, they had crossed several small streams over which the Hudson Bay Company had constructed bridges for the passage of their sheep. Much trouble was caused by the necessity of dragging a number of their pack-horses with lassos from a miry pool into which they had plunged. At the encampment, during the night, ice made on the pools to the thickness of a quarter of an inch, and the thermometer had fallen to 26°. The soil on the Elk Mountains is hard and dry; on the ridge, rock is nowhere exposed to view, and only a few fragments of sandstone lie on the surface; where they made their descent, however, and in the banks of the streamlets, they saw the rock finely developed in horizontal layers. The soil also was more sandy and of indifferent quality, and the grass in consequence is thin and occasionally mixed with ferns.

On the 16th, they encamped on the Elk river. The hunters were successful in killing a large elk, which was brought into camp and divided. Lieutenant Emmons, Mr. Agate, and Sergeant Stearns, with a Canadian as guide, left the encampment for Fort Umpqua, which was fourteen miles distant. The country for the first five miles was hilly, with scattered patches of pines, and it appears in places to be suitable for cultivation; the rest of the distance was over a country much broken. The trail carried them over a succession of steep hills and through deep ravines, which at times appeared almost impassable to their broken-down beasts; four of which Lieutenant Emmons was taking with him to exchange. They did not reach the bank of the river opposite the fort, until between eight and nine o'clock. On the opposite side they perceived a fire, with some figures passing to and fro. By firing guns, and employing the stentorian voice of their guide, it was made known that our party was in want of two canoes to cross the river. The person in charge of the fort, Mr. Gangriere, had suffered much alarm, until he recognised the voice of Boileau, their guide, which had served to quiet him, and he at once directed the canoes to cross over; while these were sought for, the horses were hobbled, and the accoutrements made up, ready for transportation. Fort Umpqua was, like all those built in this country, enclosed by a tall line of pickets, with bastions at diagonal corners; it is about two hundred feet square, and is situated more than one hundred and fifty yards from the river, upon an extensive plain; it is garrisoned by five men, two women, and nine dogs, and contains a dwelling for the superintendent, as well as store-houses, and some smaller buildings for the officers and servants' apartments.

At the time of the visit, an unusual number of Indians of the Umpqua tribe had collected around; and Mr. Gangriere said, had shown a strong disposition to attack and burn the fort. He stated that hostility to the Company and the whites generally, arose from the losses they had met with from the small-pox, which they said had been introduced among them by the Company's parties under Michel and M'Kay; and their anger was much increased by his refusal to supply them with ammunition. So critical did he consider the state of affairs, that he was about to despatch a messenger to Vancouver, to inform Dr. M'Laughlin of his situation; he had not ventured to leave the fort for many days.

Mr. Gangriere, besides entertaining Messrs. Emmons and Agate with tea, &c., gave them an account of the dangers they had to pass through. He informed them that he had long before heard of the intended journey, through the Indians, and that the news had passed on to all the tribes, who were collecting in vast numbers to oppose their passage, having sworn vengeance against all the whites, or those connected with them. He also stated that within a short time they had murdered two half-breeds who had been living peaceably among them, but who had been formerly employed by the Hudson Bay Company. By way of making his story more credible, he said that the Shaste Indians had sent him word that they were lying in wait for the whites when they should come. Large numbers of the Umpquas, according to him, had assembled at the usual crossing, to arrest the progress of the party, and he advised Lieutenant Emmons to cross the river at a place higher up. Mr. Gangriere furthermore thought their numbers so small that he was sure they would be all killed.

Lieutenant Emmons places the fort in latitude 43° 24′ N. From the account given by Mr. Gangriere, the river pursues a northwesterly course, and runs a distance of thirty miles before it enters the sea. It is navigable from the ocean to the place where the Umpqua and Elk rivers unite, about three miles below the fort, for vessels drawing not more than six feet water. The mouth of the Umpqua offers no harbour for sea-going vessels, and has only nine feet water on its bar. Its entrance is very narrow, with low sands on the north and south sides.

The Umpqua country yields a considerable supply of furs, and principally of beaver, most of which are of small size. The regulations of the Company do not seem to be so strictly in force here as to the north of the Columbia, in relation to buying the small skins. These, I have understood, they refuse to purchase there; and every Indian who is found with a small skin is refused supplies of ammunition, which has been found sufficient to prevent the killing of the young animals. Here they also obtain from the Indians some land and sea otter, deer, and bear skins.

UMPQUA INDIAN GIRL.

Mr. Agate made a sketch of one of the girls of the Umpqua tribe, of which the above wood-cut is a copy.

The agent at this post obligingly exchanged the horses, and supplied

Lieutenant Emmons with some bear and deer skins, which several of the party were in want of to make into shirts and trousers; Dr. M'Laughlin having kindly sent Lieutenant Emmons, before he left the Willamette, a letter to his agent, desiring that he would afford the party all the assistance in his power.

Lieutenant Emmons and Mr. Agate were accommodated in the store, with beds made of blankets. After arranging them, Mr. Gangriere wished them good night, locked the door, put the key in his pocket, and went to his lodgings. In the morning, at daylight, they were released.

The day was cold, damp, and foggy, preventing them from seeing any distance from the fort. The river is here one hundred and twenty yards wide, quite rapid, filled with rocks, and only navigable for canoes. The soil in the vicinity is very good, producing plentiful crops of corn, wheat, and potatoes. In the garden attached to the fort, are grown all the common vegetables of the United States, with melons, both water and musk. Cattle are said to thrive well.

In the morning it was found that a number of the Indians had departed, which relieved the agent's fears for himself, but increased those for our party. He was satisfied that it was too small in number to pass safely through, or overcome the resistance the Indians had prepared to oppose to them.

Few of these men seem to know the reason of the whites meeting with so few mishaps in passing through an apparently hostile country; and many deem that it is owing to their own skill and prowess. The truth is, that as soon as the Indians have traded with the whites, and become dependent on them for supplies, thenceforward they can be easily controlled. If disposed to be hostile, the fort at Umpqua would offer no resistance to their attack; but they are aware that all their supplies of ammunition, tobacco, blankets, and other articles of necessity, would be at once cut off; which would reduce them to great distress. They also know, that in all probability they would receive a severe chastisement for such aggression, from an armed force that would forthwith be sent among them. The self-interest of the Indians is, therefore, the true safeguard of the white traders.

After effecting the exchange of horses, they discovered that two of those they had hobbled the evening before had escaped; after a three hours' search, they were finally found on the back-trail, several miles from the fort. About noon they set out on their return, having under their escort the Indian wife of the agent, who wished to visit the camp to consult the doctor. Their fresh horses enabled them to get over the bad road with less difficulty than they had found on their way to the fort.

The party, in the mean time, had not been idle; preparations had been made for the probable encounter with the Indians; cartridges filled, and balls run, to the amount of fifty rounds apiece; the elk and deer meat had been jerked over a slow fire, and put into packs for transportation.

The examination of the country surrounding the camp, engaged the attention of the naturalists; many seeds and plants were collected. A species of oak, new to our gentlemen, was first seen here: in its size and appearance, it resembles that of the Willamette, excepting the lobes of the leaves, which have a spire at their termination; and the acorns, which are larger and more deeply set in the cup. A yellow honeysuckle was also found on the banks of the river.

The bed of the river is here composed of sandstone and clay-slate; a few hundred yards higher up the stream, the slate disappears, and beyond it is found basalt. The basaltic hills are only half a mile distant from the sandstone range which they had just passed. A few nodules of limestone, similar to that found around Astoria, occur in the shale. This rock contains a few fossils, and the sandstone exhibits some indistinct impressions of vegetables, and seams of coal or lignite. Mr. Dana, however, is of opinion that it is not probable a large deposit of the last-named mineral will be found here.

Many friendly Indians had come into the camp, who reported that the hostile tribes were preparing to attack them and dispute their passage. Some alarm seems to have existed among the trappers which manifested itself in sullenness, accompanied with threats of leaving the party. The ostensible reason for their dissatisfaction was that they were not permitted to fire their pieces at all times about the camp. Their real motive was the hope of retarding our party until it should be overtaken by the Company's trappers under Michel, who were about sixty in number. Boileau's fears had been so worked upon that he determined to leave his wife at Fort Umpqua until Michel should pass by. As usual, they suffered some detention in the morning from the straying of their horses.

Soon after leaving their camp, Corporal Hughes was taken with such a violent chill, that he was unable to proceed. The doctor, with a party under Mr. Colvocoressis, waited until the chill had subsided, and then rejoined the party.

Their guide now expressed to Lieutenant Emmons his desire to leave the party, on the plea of solicitude for his little child, but, in reality, because they were now about entering into the hostile country. After some talk, however, his fears were quieted, and he consented to go on.

During the day they passed over some basaltic hills, and then descended to another plain, where the soil was a fine loam. The prairies were on fire across their path, and had without doubt been lighted by the Indians to distress our party. The fires were by no means violent, the flames passing but slowly over the ground, and being only a few inches high.

They encamped on Billey's Creek, named after a man who had been killed here by a grisly bear, whilst passing through with a party belonging to the Company. Large game was seen in abundance, and Guardipii brought in an elk as large as a good-sized horse.

On the 19th, Burrows and his squaw, who had the night before made up their minds to leave the party, determined to continue with it. Lieutenant Emmons, in order to avoid any chance of an encounter, now deviated from the direct road, and took the upper ford or pass across the Umpqua, as he had every reason to believe that the Indians had made preparations at the lower one to obstruct his passage. About noon they reached the north fork of the Umpqua, and succeeded in fording it without accident, though they experienced some difficulty in consequence of its rapid current and uneven slippery bottom. Its breadth is about eighty yards, between banks from fifteen to twenty feet high; its depth varies from one to five feet.

As many of the party were very unwell, Lieutenant Emmons determined to halt, and the party encamped in a beautiful oak grove. With the geological features of the country, the botany had also changed; and this was also found to be the case with the animals. A new shrub was met with, resembling the shrubby geranium of Hawaii. A beautiful laurel (Laurus ptolemii,) with fragrant leaves; a Ceanothus, with beautiful sky-blue flowers of delightful frangrance; a tobacco plant (Nicotiana), of fetid odour, with white flowers. For further information, I must refer to the Botanical Report.

On the Umpqua, the first grisly bears were seen; here also the white-tailed deer was lost sight of, and the black-tailed species met with. Elk were seen in great numbers.

Two Indians made their appearance on the opposite bank of the river, and were desirous of coming into the camp; but deeming that their object was to spy out the strength of the party, it was thought more prudent not to permit this; they were accordingly motioned off. At this encampment, the horses fared badly; for it became necessary to fetter them to prevent them from being stolen, as these Indians are notorious thieves.

On the 20th, they resumed their route at an early hour, and passed, during the day, through valleys and over narrow plains, that afforded good pasturage for cattle. In the course of two hours, they reached the south fork of the Umpqua, which is similar in character to the northern.

During this day's ride, they saw one grisly bear, and had an encounter with another. On the first being perceived, chase was given, but he escaped, and while pursuing him, the second was seen. He was of large size, and approached within one hundred yards of the party, in their usual slow pace. As they came nearer to him, he raised himself on his hind quarters, and looked, with a cool indifference, upon the party. Mr. Peale dismounted and fired at him, upon which he ran off, under a shower of balls from the rest of the party, many of which hit him. They did not, however, succeed in killing him, and he finally made his escape.

They encamped on the south branch of the Umpqua river, after having passed along its eastern bank for some miles.

On the 21st, their route along the bank of the stream was through a country of the same description as before. They were approaching gradually the Umpqua Mountains, and stopped at the place where it is usual to encamp, previous to making the ascent. During the day they passed several deserted Indian huts, and met with some Indians, who were desirous of joining the camp. They declared themselves friendly to the whites, and were anxious to obtain powder and ball, which, however, were not furnished them. They were armed with guns, bows, and arrows, and were very particular in their inquiries about the time that Michel's party was to be expected.

During the night, an armed Indian was found lurking about the camp. He was recognised as an acquaintance by Warfields, one of the trappers; and on expressing his desire to accompany the party to California, permission to do so was given him by Lieutenant Emmons.

It now became evident that the Indians were on the watch to take advantage of any want of vigilance. The trappers had all become contented, and seemed quite willing to do their duty. They well knew that they had now entered a hostile country, and that it would be dangerous for any one to straggle or desert.

On the 22d, they began their route across the Umpqua Mountains. The ascent was at first gradual and easy; the path was quite narrow, and lined with dense underbrush, through which they were at times obliged to cut their way. The party were obliged to follow each other, and formed a line of nearly a mile in length. The path was continually rising and falling, until they came to a steep bank, ascending very abruptly to the height of one thousand feet. This occasioned many of the pack-horses to stumble, but without any material accident.

On the top was a small grassy plain, along which they travelled for a short distance, after which they descended rapidly into a valley where water was found. The most difficult part of the day's journey was the ascent from this valley, to effect which they toiled for three hours. The woods had been lately on fire here, and many of the trees were still ignited. This fire had evidently been lighted by the Indians for the purpose of causing the trees to fall across the path; they had also tied some of the branches together, and interlocked others. Every thing was charred, and the more annoying on that account, as our people were completely covered with charcoal dust. From the summit of this ridge, a view is had of a confused mass of abrupt ridges, between which lie small and secluded valleys. The whole range is thickly wooded, with a variety of trees, among which are the Pinus Lambertiana, (the first time it had been met with it,) Oaks, Arbutus, Prunus, Cornus, Yews, Dogwood, Hazel, Spiræa, and Castanea. In different directions, dense smoke was seen arising, denoting that these savages were on the watch for the party, and making signals to muster their forces for an attack, if a favourable opportunity should offer.

The Pinus Lambertiana, of Douglass, was not found quite so large as described by him. The cones, although fourteen inches long, were small in circumference.

They encamped on the plain of the Shaste country, which is divided by the mountains which they had passed, from the Umpqua Valley. The greatest elevation of those mountains, by the boiling temperature of water, was one thousand seven hundred and fifty feet. On reaching the encampment, it was discovered that Mr. Peale had met with the loss of a considerable part of his luggage, in consequence of the pack having been torn open by the bushes. It was therefore resolved to remain half a day at this place, in order to send back and seek for it, as well as to give the horses time to recover from the fatigue they had undergone. The 23d was therefore passed quietly, while a small division went back to search for the missing articles; but the only one which they succeeded in finding, was the camera lucida. Some Indians were met with, who no doubt had picked up all the rest of the missing articles; but as their language was unintelligible to the guides, no questions could be asked, nor any information received from them.

The rocks in this neighbourhood are here and there intersected with veins of quartz, and masses of that mineral are found strewn over the whole country. The soil that lies above the talcose rock is gravelly, and generally of a red brick-colour. Our botanists collected, during the day, many seeds. In the way of plants, they found the bulb which is used in California in the place of soap.

Their journey was resumed at an early hour on the 24th. The route passed through thickets, and in some places they discovered the fresh track of Indians, in searching for whom they discovered three squaws, who had been left when the others fled. It thus appeared that the Indians were watching them closely, and it was certain that in this country, a very small number of them would have been able to cut off the whole party without much injury to themselves, if they had possessed any courage.

The greater part of the day's journey was over undulating hills; and after making a distance of twenty-three miles, they encamped on Young's creek. This is a run of water, a few yards wide and a foot or less deep; it may be traced for a long distance by the trees which border it. They had now reached the country of the Klamet Indians, better known as the Rogues or Rascals, which name they have obtained from the hunters, from the many acts of villany they have practised. The place of encampment was only a short distance from that where Dr. Bailey was defeated.

On the 25th they continued their journey over a country resembling that traversed the day before, with the exception that the wood was not so thick. The Pinus Lambertiana was more common; the trees of this species were not beyond the usual size of the pine tribe, but their cones were seen fifteen inches in length. Some of the sugar produced by this tree was obtained: it is of a sweet taste, with a slightly bitter and piny flavour; it resembles manna, and is obtained by the Indians by burning a cavity in the tree, whence it exudes. It is gathered in large quantities. This sugar is a powerful cathartic, and affected all the party who partook of it; yet it is said that it is used as a substitute for sugar among the trappers and hunters. The soil passed over was loose and light, approaching a sandy loam.

In the afternoon they entered on the plains of Rogues' or Tootoo-tutnas river, and encamped on its banks. This is a beautiful stream, upwards of one hundred yards in width, with a rapid current, flowing over a gravelly bottom at the rate of three miles an hour: it abounds in fish, on which the Indians principally subsist; the banks are low and overgrown with bushes for some distance from the stream; the soil is poor and sandy. Two or three hundred yards from the river there is a sudden rise of ten feet, and another at the same distance beyond, from the last of which the land rises into hills from six hundred to a thousand feet in height. On these hills the soil changes to granitic sand.

Inass, the Indian hunter, being in search of game at some distance from the camp, killed a deer, and while in the act of skinning it, was surprised by a party of Indians, who shot a flight of arrows over him; he at once sprang to his horse, seized his rifle, and, according to his own account, killed one of them. The utmost haste was necessary to effect his escape, and he left his game behind.

Towards night, a canoe with two Indians approached the camp, which they were not suffered to enter. These canoes were dug out square at each end, and quite rude.

In the morning they found within their camp an Indian basket with roots, which they supposed to have been left there during the night by some Indian whose curiosity was so great as to induce him to peril his life to satisfy it.

The 26th, they passed along the banks of the Rogues' river, which runs on in a westerly direction; upon it the Indians were seen spearing salmon from their canoes.

Within a short distance of their camping-place, they came upon a party of about fifty Indians, who seemed to be surprised that their hiding-place had been discovered. They appeared to be unarmed, and looked very innocent.

During the day, their course was northeasterly, along the banks of the river. About a mile from the camp, granite of a light colour and a fine grain, that would serve as a beautiful building-stone, was seen in places. As they proceeded, the valley of the river was encroached upon by the mountains, and the ground became very much broken. The river, also, flowed in rapids, owing to the same cause, and its banks became projecting and jagged rocks. A place was pointed out where a former party had been attacked and defeated with great loss, in consequence of the Indians being able to conceal themselves behind the rocks. Our party found no one to oppose their passage. In the afternoon they reached the forks, and took the southern one, which brought them to Turner's encampment, where his party were attacked, and most of them massacred. They had allowed the Indians to enter the camp in numbers, when they suddenly rose upon the whites, who were but nine in all, and were, at the time of the attack, attending to the horses. Two of the party were killed immediately. Turner, who was a strong athletic man, was seated by the fire when the fray began; he snatched up a brand, and defended himself, dealing destruction around him, until his wife brought him his rifle, with which he killed several. A large fallen tree lies near the spot, at one end of which Turner stood, while the Indians occupied the other, and whence, assisted by his wife, he made such havoc among them, that they at last retreated, and allowed Turner and his wounded companions to make good their retreat to the north. They returned to Willamette with the loss of all their horses and property. There are still human bones, and among them parts of skulls, that mark the spot where this deadly strife took place.

Two Indians came into the camp, who were said to be friendly, having often visited the Company's parties. One of them had a kind of coat of mail, to protect himself from arrows. It resembled a strait-jacket, and only covered the body, leaving the arms free. It was made of sticks as large as a man's thumb, woven together so closely as to resist the force of arrows. It consisted of two parts, fastened together with shoulder-straps at the top, and secured around the waist at the bottom.

On the opposite bank of the Rogues' river some Indians were seen at a fire; but on the discovery of our party, they removed farther from the river. Shortly afterwards, a small dog belonging to them came down to the river bank, when a man, by the name of Wood, took his rifle, and, contrary to the orders and rules of the camp, shot it. Lieutenant Emmons had discharged the man a few days before for some misbehaviour, and he would have been turned out of camp, if there had been any place of safety for him. It was now sufficiently evident why the Indians had removed immediately out of gunshot. During the night, the Indians collected within hearing of the camp, and had a war-dance.

Most of the gentlemen of the party had suffered exceedingly from attacks of the ague; the chills were very violent while they lasted, and several were obliged to stop for an hour or two during their continuance. This became a source of uneasiness to the whole party; for it was necessary to pass on rapidly, and not delay the main body more than was unavoidably necessary: the sudden and great atmospheric changes which constantly occurred, tended to aggravate, if they did not produce, these attacks: the thermometer during the day frequently standing above 80°, and at night nearly as low as the freezing point.

On the 27th, they proceeded along the bank of the river. The Indians were observed to be gathering, and were heard to utter yells, on the opposite bank. After a while, a large band of them were seen near a rocky point which encroaches upon the river, and where the path came within the reach of their arrows. The party now had strong reason for apprehending an attack; Lieutenant Emmons, therefore, took such precautions as were necessary to clear the path from any dangers, by throwing a detachment on foot in advance of the main party. Here the high perpendicular bank confined the path to very narrow limits, rendering a passing party liable to be seriously molested by an attack from Indians, who might conceal themselves from view among the rocks on the opposite side of the rapid and narrow river. No attack, however, took place, as the Indians perceived the disposition that was made to prevent it. After the party had gone by and were beyond rifle-shot, they again made their appearance, and began to utter taunts, which were coolly listened to, except by the females of Mr. Walker's family. The squaws (wives of the hunters) had prepared themselves for an attack, apparently with as much unconcern as their husbands. Michel La Framboise with his party had been twice assaulted at this place. A few miles beyond they left the banks of the Rogues' river, taking a more easterly route, over a rolling prairie which is bounded by low hills, resembling the scenery of the Willamette Valley. The soil, in some few places, was good; but generally gravelly and barren. On the plain, some Indians were seen at a distance, on horseback, who fled like wild animals the moment they discovered the party. Some of the horses began now to give out, and they were obliged to abandon them. In the afternoon, they encamped on Beaver creek, so named by Lieutenant Emmons, from the number of those animals that were seen engaged in building dams.

An antelope was killed, which was one of four that the hunters had seen; it was of a dun and white colour, and its hair was remarkably soft. The Indians take this animal by exciting its curiosity: for this purpose they conceal themselves in a bush near its feeding-grounds, and making a rustling noise, soon attract its attention, when it is led to advance towards the place of concealment, until the arrow pierces it. If there are others in company, they will frequently remain with the wounded until they are all in like manner destroyed. This species of antelope, according to the hunters, only inhabit the prairie, being seldom seen even in the open wooded country. The flavour of the meat was thought to be superior to that of the deer.

A species of rabbit or hare was seen in great numbers on the high prairie; their large ears had somewhat the appearance of wings. The Indian mode of capturing them is by constructing a small enclosure of brush, open on one side, and having a small hole through the opposite side, into which they are driven.

It was observed too that many of the pine trees had their bark pierced in many places, with cylindrical holes about an inch and a half deep. In some of these an acorn, with its cup end inwards, was inserted, which was supposed to be the provision stored away by some species of woodpecker.

On the 28th, they advanced to the foot of the Boundary Range, where they encamped. The soil and country resembled that passed over the day before, and the woods were also oak and pine, but none of the Lambertiana. On the hills granite is seen to crop out, and in the distance was observed a singular isolated rock, which stands like a tower on the top of the ridge, rising above the surrounding forest with a bare and apparently unbroken surface. This peak, according to Lieutenant Emmons's observations, is on the parallel of 42° N.; from its top an extensive country is overlooked, and as soon as the party came in sight of it a dense column of smoke arose, which was thought to be a signal made by the Klamet Indians, to the Shaste tribe, of the approach of our party.*

On the way, they met an old squaw, with a large firebrand in her hand, with which she had just set the grass and bushes on fire; when surprised, she stood motionless, and appeared to be heedless of any thing that was passing around her. She was partly clothed in dressed deer-skins, one around her waist and another thrown over her shoulders, both fastened with a girdle, and having long fringes made of thongs of deer-skins braided; there were no other Indians in sight. The party encamped in a valley among the hills, in which were found many boulders of granite and syenite.

The hostility of the Indians, and their having been successful in stealing the horses of former parties, induced Lieutenant Emmons to have an unusually strict guard kept during the night.†

On the 29th, they set out to ascend the Boundary Mountains, which separate Mexico from the United States. It is a range of hills from twelve hundred to two thousand feet high, some of whose summits have a mural front; the features of all the ridges wear a basaltic appearance, though some of them are of sandstone, and contain fossils. As they ascended, they every moment expected to be attacked, particularly at a steep and narrow path, where a single horse has barely room to pass. The man Tibbats was one of a party of fifteen, which was defeated here by the Indians, some three years before. One of their number was killed, and two died of their wounds on the Umpqua, whither they were obliged to retreat, although they had forced the Indians back with great loss. He showed great anxiety to take his revenge on them, but no opportunity offered, for the party had no other difficulty than scrambling up a steep path, and through thick shrubbery, to reach the top. Not an

---

* This I have designated as Emmons's Peak, after the officer who had charge of this party, as a memorial of the value of his services in conducting it safely through this hostile country.

† The Klamet Indians took the pains to send word to Fort Umpqua, that they were prepared to kill any whites who should attempt to pass through their country.

Indian was to be seen, although they had evidently made some preparations to attack the party; the ground had been but recently occupied,
some large trees felled across the path by burning, and many other
impediments placed to prevent the party from advancing. The whole
mountain side was admirably adapted for an ambuscade.

At the summit of this range, they got their first view of the Klamet
Valley. It was beneath them, walled on both sides by high basaltic
hills, one beyond another. Mount Shaste, a high, snowy peak, of a
sugar-loaf form, which rose through the distant haze, bore southward,
forty-five miles distant. They descended on the south side, and
encamped on the banks of Otter creek, within a mile of the Klamet
river.

This ridge divides the waters flowing to the north and south. The
soil seemed to change for the worse, becoming more sandy.

In consequence of the illness of some of the party, it was concluded
to remain stationary on the 30th: the others made excursions around
the camp. The country they saw was a broad prairie valley, dotted
with oaks and pines, with a serpentine line of trees marking the edges
of the streams till they are lost in the distance. This valley lies in the
midst of hills, clothed with a forest of evergreens, and through this the
waters of the Klamet flow, passing beyond it, through a narrow valley
on the west. The most remarkable object in this place is the isolated
conical peak, which rises immediately from the level plain to the
height of one thousand feet, and is destitute of trees, except on its
summit.

Near their camp was the remains of an Indian hut, which had been
constructed of bent sticks: this is represented at the end of the chapter.

Lieutenant Emmons, during the day, obtained both dip and intensity
observations. The thermometer, in the shade, rose to 100°. At
dawn the following morning, it was 32°. The hunters did not succeed
in procuring any game.

On the 1st of October, they were enabled to take an early start.
The weather was, however, sultry, and the atmosphere again so smoky
as to shut out the Shaste Peak from view. In about two hours they
crossed the Klamet river, where it was about eighty yards wide, with
low banks, destitute of bushes. It was about four feet deep, with a
pebbly bottom. Both above and below the ford, there were rapids;
the volume of water was about equal to that of the Umpqua. From the
appearance of its banks, it is subject to overflow. The prairie, after
crossing the river, became dry and barren, from which a solitary bute,
by which term these hills are known, occasionally rose up, from one
to five hundred feet high. These are peculiar to this country. Heaps

of volcanic rocks, consisting of large masses of grayish or reddish porphyritic lava, in blocks of from one to ten cubic feet in size, were lying on the surface in disorderly piles. Beyond, to the eastward, the lava heaps became still more numerous.

They encamped on the southern branch of the Klamet river, which is a beautiful, clear, and rapid stream, where they met with a small spot of grass, the only one they had seen during the day. Two Indians were discovered on the look-out from one of the lava heaps. Lieutenant Emmons, taking the guide with him, succeeded in preventing their escape, and was enabled to approach them. They were at first under great fear, but soon became reconciled, and sold two salmon they had with them, which they had taken in the river with their fish-spears. The salmon were of a whitish colour, and not at all delicate to the taste; their tails were worn off, and the fish otherwise bruised and injured. Many salmon are caught in all these rivers. The Indians were thought to be better-looking than those before seen about the villages, and were quite naked, excepting the maro. After having disposed of their fish, they were willing to sell their bows and arrows, which they had hid in the grass. These which were all neatly made, were bought for a knife. They then pointed out some more of their tribe, who were seated on the side of a distant hill, and were very desirous that they might be permitted to come into the camp; but permission was refused them. Here our gentlemen saw large bundles of rushes, made up in the form of a lashed-up hammock, which the Indians are said to use instead of canoes.

On the 2d, they travelled all day over a rolling prairie, without water; the low ground was incrusted with salts, notwithstanding which, the land was better than that passed over the day before. Some patches of spiræa and dogwood were met with, and a better growth of grass; although it was still very scanty.

Large herds of antelopes were seen, but none of them were killed; the hunters also recognized the mountain sheep, which are of a dark colour, much larger than the common sheep, and having large horns. Towards the afternoon they came to some holes containing water; and such had been the suffering of some of the animals from thirst, that they rushed into them with their packs, and it required much labour to extricate them, for which purpose it was necessary to use the lasso. About midday they left the Klamet Valley, which is far inferior to any portion of the country they had passed through; and as they crossed the hills which enclose it, they found that the out-cropping rocks were composed of a dark green serpentine. They encamped a little beyond the hills, and in the vicinity of their camp, boulders of a coarse syenite, forming the bed of the creek, and lying along its course, were seen. The hornblend crystals of the latter rock were often two inches long, and were set in a white granular paste of feldspar.

At their camp they were visited by a party of Shaste Indians, who were allowed to enter it, and for some time there was a brisk trade for their bows and arrows. These Indians are a fine-looking race, being much better proportioned than those more to the northward, and their features more regular. One of the boys was extremely good-looking. He had a bright black eye, and pleasing expression of countenance; he was clad in dressed deer-skins, over his shoulders and about his body, but his legs were bare. They all wore their black hair hanging down to their shoulders; and they do not compress their heads. Mr. Agate had much difficulty in getting them to stand still for the purpose of having their portraits taken, and gave them a miniature of his mother to look at, hoping that this would allay their fears, but it had a contrary effect, as they now believed that he desired to put some enchantment upon them, and thought that he was the medicine-man of the party.

They obtained an exhibition of the archery of the Indians by putting up a button at twenty yards distance, which one of them hit three times out of five: the successful marksman was rewarded with it and a small piece of tobacco. They use these bows with such dexterity as to kill fish, and lanch their arrows with such force, that one of the gentlemen remarks he would as leave be shot at with a musket at the distance of one hundred yards, as by one of these Indians with his bow and arrow. Their bows and arrows are beautifully made: the former are of yew and about three feet long; they are flat, and an inch and a half to two inches wide: these are backed very neatly with sinew, and painted. The arrows are upwards of thirty inches long; some of them were made of a close-grained wood, a species of spiræe, while others were of reed; they were feathered for a length of from five to eight inches, and the barbed heads were beautifully wrought from obsidian: the head is inserted in a grooved piece, from three to five inches long, and is attached to the shaft by a socket; this, when it penetrates, is left in the wound when the shaft is withdrawn; a very shallow blood-channel is sometimes cut in the shaft. In shooting the arrow, the bow is held horizontally, braced by the thumb of the left hand, and drawn by the thumb and three first fingers of the right hand. To obviate the disadvantage of drawing to the breast, the chest is thrown backwards; on discharging the arrow, they throw out the right leg and stand on the left. Their quivers are made of deer, raccoon, or wild-cat skin; these skins are generally whole, being left open at the tail end.

A disease was observed among them which had the appearance of the leprosy, although the doctor did not recognise it is such, one of the six had wasted away to almost a skeleton from its effects.

The old man was pointed out as the father-in-law of Michel La Framboise, who, as I have said before, has a wife in nearly every tribe.

As to dress, they can scarcely be said to wear any except a mantle of deer or wolf skin. A few of them had deer-skins belted around their waists with a highly ornamented girdle.

On the 3d, they continued their route up the plain, and soon reached its termination, after which they entered the forest on the slopes of the Shaste Range; the path was rendered very broken and uneven by the knolls of trachyte which were seen in every direction. On arriving at the top of the ridge, they had a magnificent view of the snowy peak of Shaste, with a nearer and intermediate one destitute of snow, with tall pines growing nearly to its top. Where the surface could be seen, it appeared as though it was covered with large blocks of rock: its conical shape proved its volcanic character, although no crater could be perceived.

The Shaste Peak is a magnificent sight, rising as it does to a lofty height, its steep sides emerging from the mists which envelope its base, and seem to throw it off to an immense distance; its cleft summit gave proof of its former active state as a volcano. The snow lies in patches on the sides and part of the peak of this mountain; but there is a great difference in the position of its snow-line from that of Mount Hood or St. Helen's. Its height is said to be fourteen thousand three hundred and ninety feet, but Lieutenant Emmons thinks it is not so high. After passing this ridge, they soon met the head waters of the Sacramento, flowing to the southward, and their camp was pitched on the banks of another stream, that came from the Shaste Peak.

Our party now had their prospects somewhat brightened, having passed safely through the country of the "Bad Indians." I cannot but regret that they should at this time have been found in so hostile a state that it rendered it not only prudent, but necessary for the safety of the party, that all intercourse should be avoided, and consequently one of the objects of the Expedition, that of acquiring some knowledge of their actual conditions, numbers, &c., was frustrated.

On the 4th, they had fairly entered into the district of pines: again some of the Lambertiana were measured, and found to be eighteen feet in circumference, with cones sixteen inches long.

They encamped on Destruction river, which runs from this mountain range toward the south, in a place where they found food for their horses and water in abundance. The air was delightful; the forest protected them from the rays of the sun, and besides this the game was plentiful. Near the encampment, in a northwest direction, was a mountain ridge shooting up in sharp conical points and needle-shaped peaks, having a precipitous front. One of these peaks almost overhangs the valley, presenting a gray surface of naked rock two thousand feet high. The valley which adjoins is strewn over with boulders of white granite, similar to that already described. From this, there is little doubt that the ridge is formed of the same material. At meridian they reached a small valley bordering on the Destruction river, where they found a chalybeate spring. The water oozes out from the rocks, bubbling up freely, and is highly charged with carbonic acid gas. In taste it was found agreeable to both the riders and the animals. Its temperature was 50°, that of the air being 75°; about a gallon per minute is discharged. Around it there is a thick deposit of iron rust, and a few yards distant a small pond, the bottom of which was also coated with a ferruginous deposit. The rocks in the vicinity of the spring were of the trachytic and slightly cellular lava, which is speckled with grains of feldspar. The hunters said that the spring was in all respects similar to that on the Bear creek, which empties into the Youta Lake, known in the Rocky Mountains as the Soda Spring. Mr. Dana found some difficulty in accounting for this emission of carbonic acid, as no limestone was found or known to exist in the neighbourhood; yet he is inclined to believe, that it may be owing to the decomposition of sulphuret of iron. For further information upon this subject, I would refer to his Geological Report.

On this night they had a severe storm from the westward, and occasionally heard the crash produced by the falling of large pines.

The character of the country had now changed, and afforded a new and more extended botanical field, as well as new geological features. The general tendency of the ridges is north and south, but the whole may be classed as a series of valleys and hills thrown in all positions. The hills are, for the greater part, covered with soil, when it can find any place of deposit; and all are richly clothed with vegetation. The principal timber consists of pines and oaks; and there are many smaller plants, of which the flowers must be abundant in the proper season. As it was, our botanists reaped something of a harvest; for information respecting which, the Botanical Report is referred to.

They continued to follow Destruction river until the 9th, when it was joined by a stream from the northward and eastward, which was taken to be the northeast branch of Pitt river: it was larger than the stream they had been following for the last few days, and is supposed by some to take its rise in Pitt Lake; but this I very much doubt, as it lies on the other side of the Cascade or Californian Range, and the two united form the Sacramento.

Though I have dignified these two streams with the name of rivers, it must not be supposed that they are really such, in our acceptation of the word. The party are generally of the opinion that they should be called creeks.

They encamped late in the evening near a small rivulet, to the westward of the Sacramento. They had much difficulty with their horses, which had now become tired out. For this reason it became necessary to abandon one of them, as he was unable to proceed any further.

On the 10th they made an early start, and left the mountains. The width of the range they had passed through was upwards of one hundred miles. At one place Guardipii, their guide, lost his way; but on applying to Warfields' Indian wife, she pointed out the trail without difficulty.

They had now passed into the Sacramento Valley, and had met with some of the Kinkla tribe of Indians, who were known to be friendly, and they became relieved from anxiety. The botanical character of the landscape changed as suddenly: instead of firs, pines, &c., they found themselves among sycamores, oaks, and cotton-wood trees. The oaks bear a variety of acorns, which are equally the food of the bears and the Indians. The prairie bordering the Sacramento at this place is about fifty feet below the upper prairie, and continues for many miles very regularly on the same level; the latter falling into it by a sloping bank.

SACRAMENTO INDIAN.

In the evening the camp was visited by many of these friendly and docile Indians, who made themselves quite easy, laughing and joking, and appeared rather to look upon the party as beneath them. They had some resemblance to the Shaste Indians; most of them were naked; the others had a piece of deer-skin thrown over their shoulders; their faces were marked with an expression of good humour. Some of them wore their hair long, extending below the neck and divided from the top; in others, and most commonly, it was drawn back and gathered in a bunch behind, where it was fastened with a string of deer-sinew; their ears were bored, and a short string inserted with a few beads; the face was usually painted, the upper part of the cheek in the form of a triangle, with a blue-black substance, mixed with some shiny particles that resembled pulverized mica.

The Indians were darker as to colour than the northern tribes, and their general appearance resembled that of the South Sea islanders. Their food consists principally of fish and acorns; of the latter they make a kind of black cake by shelling the acorns, drying them in the sun, and then pounding them between stones to a meal, which they mix with a little water and arbutus-berries, which gives it a flavour; it is then formed into cakes about two inches thick, when it is wrapped in leaves and baked; it is quite black and eats like cheese: these acorns are quite palatable in the raw state. The seeds of the different genus of pine are also eaten, particularly one that is peculiar to California. The arbutus-berry is in great plenty, and is also ground into meal; they have also many grapes. The game had also become very abundant, in consequence of the quantities of food, which attracts them as well as the Indians, and many antelopes and deer were observed. Large flocks of California partridges and geese were seen: among the birds was a new species of magpie.

None of the Indians but men visited the camp, the women being left at their rancheria. Our party went to visit it; it was about half a mile below the camp, and consisted of some rude huts, built of poles, and divided by coarse mats into a number of small apartments. The whole was surrounded by a brush fence, which served for a stockade.

The huts were small in size and devoid of comfort or cleanliness. It was remarked that the women were much inferior to the men in personal appearance, looking careworn and wrinkled, probably from hard work; for on them seems to depend the preparation of all their winter's supply of food, at which they seemed to be constantly engaged; while the men are to be seen lounging about, or engaged in games of hazard. They are, however, during the season, engaged in taking salmon, either in weirs, or by spearing: the former method has been described already; for the latter they use a long forked spear or fish-gig, which has a sharp deer's horn to confine the two prongs, and is attached to the spear by a small lanyard, which in entering the fish slips off, and retains its hold.

At the rancheria, several dances were performed; and it was observed that many of the women were tattooed on their arms and body.

On reaching the Sacramento, it had been recommended to Lieutenant Emmons to procure canoes, if possible, either by purchase or constructing them, in consequence of the belief that both his party and the animals would have been nearly if not quite worn out. No canoes, however, were to be found, and, as has been seen in my account of that river, none were used by the Indians. Neither could any timber be obtained without much detention, of which to construct one. It was, therefore, necessary for him to keep on to Captain Suter's, where he expected to find boats to take them to the ship as soon as possible. From what Lieutenant Emmons could learn, there was no difficulty in proceeding in canoes from this place, though there would have been some obstacles to surmount, particularly the fish-weirs, which exist below.

On the 11th, they took leave of the friendly Indians, who had, during the night, been as watchful as themselves, passing the word among their look-outs as if they had been regular sentinels. The party proceeded down the western bank of the Sacramento, over a rolling prairie country, which they characterize as the most worthless they had met with. The soil consists of gravel, coarse pebbles, and large stones, mixed with sand. They frequently met the beds of streams, three hundred yards wide, which intersect this part of the country, the pebbles in which are chiefly composed of jasper and milky quartz, with a few of basalt, pudding-stone, and pieces of slate. They made this day, twenty-five miles—the longest day's ride on the journey.

On the 12th, Lieutenant Emmons determined to ford the river, as it was doubtful whether he would have so good an opportunity lower down. Inass, one of the hunters, was found sitting beside his horse, on the opposite side of the ford, loaded with the meat and skin of a large grisly bear which he had killed. The river was about three feet deep, and two hundred yards wide. They stopped at a place known among the hunters as Bear-camp, from the number of grisly bears found here. Five of them were shot the same afternoon, with three deer, which were seen feeding within sight of the camp, all in excellent condition. The country on the east side of the river was more level than on the west, and the soil was thought to be better. Few plants, however, were seen, in consequence of the country having been burned over.

The country continued much the same until, on the 15th, they came in sight of the Prairie Butes, a regular collection of hills, rising out of the level plain like islands from the water. These are very deceptive in height, and may be seen from a great distance. The party encamped on a small creek, called by the trappers the Little Fork of the Butes. The hunters said that the party employed by the Hudson Bay Company last year caught more than one hundred beavers during their sojourn in this neighbourhood with their cattle.

On the 16th, they passed towards the Butes, and encamped, after an ineffectual search for water, at a place that had been occupied for the same purpose by Michel, in the valley or "Kraal" of the Butes. Here they found two deep holes of stagnant water, the remains of a rivulet that was now dried up. The ground around and near the Butes is covered with a great quantity of the bones of animals that resort hither for safety during the season of the freshets which flood the whole of this extensive plain. The soil is quite loose and crusted over with the deposit left by the water, through which the horses broke to the depth of four or five inches; nearer the Butes, the soil is harder and strewed with fragments of volcanic rocks. There is little doubt that each of the Butes was once a volcano. They are grouped within an oval space, which has a circumference of about thirty miles: the longest diameter of the oval figure lies in a northeast and southwest direction. The valley passes through the southern part, and opens out on the eastern: it is about seven miles in length; and here the party found water. This valley may be considered almost as a prolongation of the exterior plain, though parts of it are somewhat higher, as appeared by its not having been overflowed. The highest of the Butes was made, by a triangulation executed by Lieutenant Emmons and Mr. Eld, seventeen hundred and ninety-four feet. They have the appearance of having once been much higher and more extended than they now are. The volcanic rock, according to Mr. Dana, is a trachytic porphyry, of a purplish colour, which contains hornblend and six-sided tables of mica, with glassy feldspar, in crystals from a quarter to half an inch in size, disseminated through it; some of the rocks have a porcelain aspect, but this variety only constitutes a few of the peaks. The rock is found either in horizontal or vertical layers or curved in all directions, and is thickly sprinkled with mica. The Butes were ascertained to be in the latitude of 39° 08' N.; yet it has been generally believed that these were on the dividing line between Oregon and California.

On the 17th, they proceeded, and in about fifteen miles they found themselves on the banks of the Feather river. There is a difficulty in fording this stream, on account of the quicksands; and the first time they attempted it, the guide and his horse were nearly lost. To swim the river was equally impracticable, in the weak and worn-out state of their animals. They therefore proceeded down its bank, looking for a ford. On their way, Inass killed a wild cow, one of a herd of ten. It is said that the wild cattle, which have originated from the animals that have escaped from the herds passing through the country to Oregon, are increasing very fast.

They encamped in a beautiful oak grove, near the junction of the Feather river with the Sacramento. The two rivers are of about the same size, being each seventy yards wide. The waters of the Feather are clear, and in many places deep; the banks are, as usual, lined with sycamore, cotton-wood, and oak, and were at this time about twenty-five feet above the stream. It appears to be navigable for boats. The party succeeded in fording it on the 18th, within two miles of the junction. Near the ford, the Indians had an extensive burial-ground, marked by a vast number of skulls and bones, that lie scattered around in all directions, and are said to be all that remains of a once powerful tribe, that has been swept off by disease.

They then proceeded on to Captain Suter's, where they arrived the next day.

The officers appear to have entered this valley with a high idea of its fruitfulness, and with the expectation of finding the soil abounding with every thing that could make it desirable for the abode of the agriculturist, and susceptible of producing all that can add to the comfort or convenience of man. It is not surprising that they should have been sadly disappointed, when they beheld a large part of it barren, and destitute even of pasturage, while that which is fertile is liable to be annually overflowed. The high prairie is equally gravelly and unfertile. Yet it is necessary to say there is a sufficient quantity of good soil to make it a valuable agricultural country, and that it would be capable of affording subsistence to a large number of inhabitants, more, however, from the extraordinary fertility of these grounds than from their extent.

After leaving Captain Suter's, or New Helvetia, the party divided. The detachment under Lieutenant Emmons, with Messrs. Dana, Agate, Colvocoressis, and Dr. Whittle, embarked in the Vincennes' launch, which met them a short distance below that place, and reached San Francisco at eight o'clock P. M. on the 24th.

The other detachment, consisting of Messrs. Eld, Peale, Rich, Brackenridge, and the sergeant, with some of the men, went by land. I cannot avoid again returning my thanks to Captain Suter, for his kindness to this party. All the officers spoke most particularly of the attention he paid to them, individually and collectively, and of his care and watchfulness in making provision for our sick.

On the 21st, the land party commenced their journey, with a young and intelligent Spaniard for a guide. The same day they made fifteen miles, passing over a dry portion of country, and encamped near two ponds, called in the country, Poros, the only place, as was supposed, where water could be obtained within twenty miles; they, however, found some the next day in the Rio Cosmenes, within a mile and a half of the camp. Game was, as usual, very abundant; but the whole country was suffering from the drought that has been before spoken of.

On the 22d, about noon, they crossed the river Mogueles, which was then a small stream; but at other seasons, it is said it cannot be crossed on horseback. They travelled this day as far as the San Juan; the only water that it contained was in small pools. This place had been termed the Frenchman's Camp. The ducks and geese had rendered the water scarcely drinkable.

On the 23d, before noon, they reached the San Joachim, which they found about fifty yards wide, and about three feet deep. Under the expectation of finding water, they were induced to ride forty-four miles, but were again disappointed. On the 24th, they entered among the Pul Porrice hills, a bare and barren range, composed of sandstone and volcanic rocks. As they approached the mission of San Jose, the country became more hilly, the oak abundant, and herds of cattle and horses were seen. On their way they fell in with large encampments of Indians, who were busily employed in collecting acorns. They were all half civilized as to dress, the men being clothed in shirts and trousers, some in velvet breeches; the women in calico gowns, and gay-coloured shawls; several hundred of these were met, each loaded with the beef which is distributed to them in weekly rations. They are annually allowed a short holiday to return to their native wilds, during the time acorns are in season.

The approach to the mission shows it to have once been a large establishment. It has all the appearance of a town, being built in the form of a street of considerable length. In the centre is the church and convent, with large dwelling-houses on each side of it, and on the opposite side the houses for the neophytes, consisting of small low buildings, with every appearance of filth and decay about them. Indeed the whole establishment is falling into ruins; the walls and gates are thrown down, and every thing wears a look of neglect, both in the buildings and the persons who inhabit them. The halcyon days of this mission have passed away; it is no longer the abode of hospitality and good living, since it has fallen into the hands of the administradors or agents of the government. The remains of a fine garden are also perceptible, where there is yet good fruit; and near by are extensive fields of Indian corn, which were formerly cultivated by irrigation.

The reception of our gentlemen was in keeping with the place, neither polite nor friendly. No civilities were tendered, no offers of accommodations made, although they brought a particular letter from Captain Suter. Our party were inclined to believe that this was owing, in part at least, to the condition of their wardrobe; their whole appearance, it must be admitted, was not much in their favour, dressed as they were in the deer-skins that had been worn on their journey, yet they thought that their characters might have been discovered through their buckskins.

The administrador told them there was no accommodation for their horses, and showed them none, except a miserable hole without any furniture. The letter of introduction bore the superscription of Don Jose Antonio Estrade. They met with the tailor to the establishment, Ephraim Travel, an American, of Philadelphia, who showed them the lions of the place with great politeness, and as far as in him lay, made amends for their otherwise cold reception. He took them round the gardens, through the churches, and told them that the Indians under the care of the mission were at the present time about six hundred, which was only one-third of the number they had two years before. In consequence, there was but little cultivation carried on, compared to what there had been formerly.

The harvest at the mission had been very small, from the great drought. No rain had fallen for upwards of a year. The vintage, however, had been very fine, and forty barrels of wine had been made, besides a large supply of grapes for the whole establishment. The two vineyards comprise about four acres, and beside vines, are filled with apple, pear, and other fruit trees. The buildings of the mission are all constructed of adobes, and covered with tile roofs.

Fortunately for the party, Mr. Forbes, the agent of the Hudson Bay Company, residing a few miles farther on, happened to be at the mission, and very kindly offered them accommodations, which they thankfully accepted. They found him lodged in a comfortable two-story adobe house, situated on the border of an extensive prairie, but without any trees or cultivation around it. He entertained them very hospitably.

The party visited Santa Clara the next day, where their reception was very courteous, and furnished a strong contrast to that at San

Jose. After two days' journey, they reached Yerba Buena at noon on the 28th, having paid a visit to the mission of Nostra Señora de los Dolores, within three miles of that place.

They reached the ship the same afternoon, and though fatigued and somewhat worn down, they had been much pleased with their jaunt.

Although this journey from the Columbia to the Sacramento was attended with much fatigue, yet the labour and suffering were more than compensated by the information it furnished in relation to the southern section of Oregon, and the addition of new objects to the collections of the Expedition. Although every thing was not attained that I intended, yet I feel satisfied that all was done which the very limited time, and the hostile state of the country, would permit. To the perseverance and prudence of Lieutenant Emmons, much credit is due, as well as to the other officers and naturalists, for the manner in which they co-operated with him. The duties assigned them were performed under the most trying circumstances, while worn down by distressing attacks of the ague and fever. This disease, in particular, affected those members of the party who had been encamped on the Willamette, where it was supposed they contracted it.

The closing scene of the tour deserves a short notice, as it is probably peculiar to a country like California. On the arrival of the party, it seemed to have been surmised by the inhabitants of Yerba Buena, and by the few who dwell at the mission, presidio, and neighbouring rancheria, together with the trappers and hunters, that our horses and accoutrements must necessarily be parted with. I make no doubt that good bargains were anticipated, or rather a determination made that they would have all for little or nothing. The alcalde, the only person in authority, a man of much rotundity and little height interested himself exceedingly in the matter. In the first place, it was discovered that many of the horses were not marked, and therefore, agreeably to the laws of the country, they belonged to the government; secondly, that many of them were beyond recovery from their worn-out condition; thirdly and lastly, that if they did recover, they would be worthless. The same faults were applied to the pack-saddles, parfleshes, and appichemens, that have been described in the beginning of this chapter, and which had caused so much trouble to procure. Their value, in the eyes of these gentlemen, was next to nothing. Under these circumstances, a notice was posted up at the few corners of the pueblo of Yerba Buena, that they would be disposed of by public auction.

This attracted a great crowd, and among the number was the only representative of authority of the government, the redoubtable alcalde. The horses had been put in lots, as was likewise the case with the accoutrements. Each of these was announced first in English, then in Spanish, and last in French, which gave the auctioneer a full opportunity to descant upon their sore backs, lameness, visible ribs, and sorry appearance. The Spanish language seemed to be more copious in words to express their condition, for it certainly produced many jeers and much laughter among the motley throng. They went off briskly, however, in lots, from one dollar and fifty cents to five and six dollars each, principally under the bid of the redoubtable alcalde, who had arranged things well enough with those under his authority; but as there were some of our countrymen and foreigners there whom he could not overawe, he had to pay what was deemed a fair price for the worn-out animals, although they were sold without reserve; and when one considers that a brood-mare is valued here at less than a dollar, it will appear so. The proceeds of the sale amounted to two hundred and ten dollars.

SHASTE HUT.